THE CANADAIR ARGUS

CL-28 CP-107

THE UNTOLD STORY OF CANADA'S COLD WAR MARITIME HUNTER

Edited by Sarah Facey
Designed by Cary Baker and Cynthia McMurray
Printed and bound in Canada at Friesens

Library and Archives Canada Cataloguing in Publication

The Canadair Argus CL-28 CP 107 : The untold story of Canada's Cold War maritime hunter / compiled by Bert Campbell and Cary Baker ; illustrations by Adam Murray and Rob Arsenault.

Includes bibliographical references.
ISBN 978-1-927003-06-0

1. Canadair CP-107 Argus (Antisubmarine aircraft)--History. 2. Cold War.
I. Campbell, Bert, 1948- II. Baker, Cary, 1967-

UG1242.A25C35 2011   358.4'5   C2011-903207-4

10 9 8 7 6 5 4 3 2 1

Published in 2011 by Bryler Publications Inc.
Bryler Publications Inc.
Box 1035,
Chester, NS
B0J 1J0

www.brylerpublications.com

For my Dad, Captain Gary Herman Baker CD – Argus Pilot
May 01, 1940 – Jan 20, 2005

"Those who flew with you still talk about your soft Argus landings!"

– Love, Cary

Another misty morning takeoff of Argus 736 from Summerside, PEI

Painting:Rob Arsenault. 2009

This book is also dedicated to the men and women who built, flew,
maintained and supported the Argus and Canadian Long Range Maritime
Patrol operations from 1958 – 1981

Bert

Foreword

With the dawn of the Aurora in 1980, a major icon of Canadian military history disappeared as if it had never been there—despite its invaluable 25-year existence. Tired and worn, fuelled by alternate 100 octane gasoline instead of its required, but no-longer-available, 115 octane and with sensors in need of updating, the venerable Argus aircraft's final humiliation was being chopped up and melted to its basic aluminum at Summerside, PEI—a base that also ceased to exist with the passing of the Argus.

A very large aircraft, the CANADAIR CL-28 (CP-107) Argus, named after the Greek monster with 100 eyes, began operations in 1958, replacing the World War II Lancaster and interim Neptune, and was a powerful force to be reckoned with. Packed with the latest electronics, with two huge weapons bays for 8,000 pounds of ordnance and enough fuel to stay airborne for more than 22 hours, this aircraft was NATO's premier patrol aircraft. With its highly-secret role, and highly classified missions, publicity was stifled, unlike the overt and glamorous public relations of fighter squadrons in Europe—where deterrence was enhanced by the known presence of large numbers of armed aircraft. The Argus missions, on the contrary, required stealthy departures at all hours, to what destination only few were privy, and returned so much later that its presence was lost among the many training aircraft at the busy airfields. For days, weeks and months on end, Argus aircraft searched, located, tracked and were prepared to destroy Soviet submarines that threatened North America. Reconnaissance of surface vessels came with the territory, as Soviet ships often accompanied the sub-surface targets, and they were a constant threat to the sea lines of communication to Europe. During the fabled Cuban missile crisis, Argus crews saw their finest hours and helped prevent a nuclear World War III—but few knew this because the Canadian government had not sanctioned their participation and their work went unpublicized until recent years. This unrelenting presence of our armed and dedicated forces, flying this marvelous aircraft, kept the Soviets at bay and played a significant part in their final fall in 1989. Because the Cold War never turned "hot", there was no actual victory declared in 1989 but, to those of us who "fought", we "won" that War. The endless and dogged determination of the Argus aircrew, ground crew and supporting agencies kept this mighty aircraft serviceable and capable through more than half the Cold War's 40-years duration.

Although the NATO role absorbed most of the Argus commitments, the Argus was a perfect Canadian aircraft. Able to fly the entire coastline, react to search-and-rescue missions anywhere in Canada, and use its sensors to affirm sovereignty in the Arctic, in the coastal economic zones or anywhere there was a need, this aircraft had unlimited uses.

Flying this aircraft was very special, although like good wine the flying improved with aging. "Engineer, wet power" were the magic words for flight engineers that we pilots used to unleash 14,800 raw horsepower that lifted 157,000 pounds of machine, men and weapons into the air. In my 42-years Air Force career, nothing curled the hair on the back of my neck like those words, and no

Dawn Patrol: The bulging chin radome of this nicely silhouetted Argus leaves no doubt that she is a Mark 1 variant. Things are unusually calm and serene from the nose lookout position high over the glinted ocean as this Maritime Patrol crew transits to their assigned patrol area for another 18 hours.

Painting: Rob Arsenault

---

aircraft I flew gave me more satisfaction of a job well done. Flying the aircraft took skill and patience and, with the choreography of a well-run crew, the experience was the epitome of a military profession.

Certain aspects of Argus operations were unique and will be forever remembered. The Argus run-up was always very special, and one that sometimes lasted an unbelievable four hours, or more. Unserviceability with this aircraft did not mean returning to the ramp, shutting down and waiting for the fix. Instead, a yellow vehicle with spare parts and technicians would appear under the wing, and the repairs would be done in situ—even at night and in bad weather. Considering that the average flight during my time was 18 hours, plus two each for briefing and debriefing, a day flying the Argus most often lasted well beyond 24 hours.

Takeoffs were straight forward, unless the day was hot and the weight was at maximum, or we were burning "soft coal" (100 octane fuel). Then the take-off run and climb to even moderate altitudes was unbelievably long–especially if taking off in Norway where it seemed mountains always appeared at the end of the runway, regardless of the takeoff direction. Once airborne, the aircraft became a hive of activity as sonobuoys were prepared for the mission, equipment was set up and checked and breakfast, lunch, dinner or between meal snacks were made available. Food was critical in sustaining crew capability on long missions, and we were well sustained and, although cooking in the galley meant hot food, as the aircraft was not pressurized or air conditioned, odours from whatever was cooked lingered forever. Those with weak stomachs suffered through meals of pork chops or fried bacon, especially when the air was rough and/or the crew was doing hard manoeuvring during "JULIE" or "SNIFFER".

Unlike its jet-engine, pressurized and air conditioned successors, the Argus could seldom climb out of bad weather, nor could it normally abort a mission for weather, and winter over the ocean was the very worst. Although the aircraft had excellent anti-icing and de-icing systems, ice accretion still occurred on parts of the airframe, providing a spectacle as most ice departed on touchdown with a mighty spray of white particulate.

Landing an Argus was another unique experience. After trimming the aircraft on final approach, the selection of full flap on late final caused the nose to drop rapidly and required an immediate three "big handfuls of elevator up trim". Slow application meant the aircraft nose would continue downward, and the excessive back pressure required on the control column usually resulted in a hard landing. Judgment of the round-out was also a finesse acquired over time; rounding out too early caused a stall on the runway, too late caused a hopping down the runway in a bogie rock; add strong cross-winds and the experience could be quite frightening. Yet, in retrospect, these idiosyncrasies were what made the aircraft special and made the acquired skill so rewarding.

Without the care, support and superb operation of this mighty submarine hunter, by literally thousands of people in a decisive quarter century, the world might well be a different place. The many who flew her may not all have loved her, but the respect for her was unanimous. The Argus was one of the greatest aircraft ever built, and I was thankful for the rich experience of flying her, operating with such professional crewmembers and being supported by some of the most dedicated and hard-working people in the Air Force.

—Major-General (Retired) Ian Patrick CD, BA

Argus Mk2 20733 from 415 "Swordfish" Squadron, based at RCAF Station Summerside, PEI, banks aggressively during a MAD run to track a submerged target during the early 1960's.

Painting: Rob Arsenault

The CL-28 (CP-107) was a new weapon built to counter a new threat

Photo: Canadian National Archives

The Argus was the first and only maritime patrol aircraft designed and built in Canada to meet unique Canadian requirements. She was a prime player in the maritime defence of North America and a valued NATO asset in maintaining the strategic balance in the North Atlantic during the Cold War. Operationally, the Argus was at the forefront of Canada's defence needs. For the first time, the Royal Canadian Air Force (RCAF) had a maritime aircraft specifically tailored to conduct surveillance over Canada's vast ocean areas of responsibility.

The Argus's exceptional range and endurance far exceeded any other NATO aircraft, giving it the ability to loiter for eight hours or more over any region of the North Atlantic without refuelling. In the late 1950's and early 1960's, the Argus was admired by Canada's allies on both sides of the Atlantic and was regarded as one of NATO's premier maritime patrol aircraft. More importantly, the Argus's advanced technology navigation and sensor systems demonstrated Canada's resolve to regain the supremacy in Anti-Submarine Warfare (ASW) that it enjoyed at the end of the Second World War, as well as being considered a valued contributor to the NATO alliance.

During the Second World War, Canada, Britain and the United States developed hard-earned expertise in ASW. This expertise was gained at the expense of heavy ship losses, but many lessons were learned. The most important lesson was that ASW aircraft required sufficient range to reach the mid-Atlantic and sufficient endurance to remain over the convoys for long periods of time. During the Battle of the Atlantic, the Allies most serious strategic liability was the inability to close the mid-Atlantic air gaps between Newfoundland and Iceland, and Iceland and Britain. These gaps allowed German U-boats to attack convoys with impunity. The lia-

B-24 Liberator VLR in RCAF livery a few years after the end of WW II
Photo: Greenwood Aviation Museum Collection

bility was not resolved until mid-1943 when the Very Long Range (VLR) B-24 Liberator was introduced into the Royal Canadian Air Force's Eastern Air Command and the Royal Air Force's (RAF's) Coastal Command.[1] The presence of VLR aircraft was directly responsible for the dramatic reduction in the devastating merchant shipping losses and, in fact, marked the turning point in the allies' fortunes in the Battle of the Atlantic. These range and endurance lessons were sagely designed into what was to become Canada's principal postwar maritime patrol aircraft, the Canadair Argus.

Sixty Lancasters were converted to the Maritime Reconnaissance Role (MR) to work cooperatively with the Royal Canadian Navy (RCN)
Photo: Greenwood Aviation Museum Collection

After victory in Europe in May 1945, eight squadrons of Canadian built Mark 10 Lancasters were transferred from the RCAF's No. 6 Bomber Group in England to four bases in Nova Scotia[2] to train for the "Tiger Force" in the war against Japan. However, the sudden collapse of Japan after the atomic bombings of Hiroshima and Nagasaki changed everything; the "Tiger Force" was disbanded and the Lancasters were placed in storage on the prairies. After the war, Canada's Navy and Air Force, which were third largest among the allies, were drastically reduced to peacetime levels. The ASW expertise that was garnered during the Battle of the Atlantic was al-

[1] Nos. 10 and 11 Bomber Reconnaissance Squadrons were the only Eastern Air Command squadrons equipped with the VLR B-24 Liberator. The squadrons operated from Dartmouth, NS and Gander and Torbay, NL.
[2] Dartmouth, 431 and 434 Squadrons; Greenwood, 405 and 408 Squadrons; Yarmouth, 419 and 428 Squadrons; Debert, 420 and 425 Squadrons.

After WW II the Soviets began an active campaign to increase surface and sub surface fleets in an attempt to dominate the international sea lanes should hostilities between NATO and the Soviets erupt.

Photo: DND

lowed to atrophy and most of the ships and aircraft that represented industrial and technical supremacy were sold to scrap dealers.

In the late 1940's, Soviet expansionism and the Berlin crisis brought deterioration to international stability. The West responded by signing the Treaty of Brussels, later becoming the Western Union Defence Organization. In mid 1949, this was enlarged to become the North Atlantic Treaty Organization (NATO). NATO would bring great expansion among Western forces and was a profound impetus to the resurrection of Canadian ASW skills. NATO doctrine provided for mutual defence among member nations and called for the security of the NATO area to be strengthened. Specific concern arose over the rapidly developing Soviet submarine threat; the Union of Soviet Socialist Republics (USSR) was building submarines by the hundreds! With Canada accepting NATO defence responsibilities for a vast area of the western North Atlantic,[3] the Canadian government embarked on a rapid expansion of its maritime forces. The RCAF resurrected its Second World War Eastern Air Command in the form of Maritime Group. Unfortunately, in the post war doldrums and the rush to clear the books of as much military equipment as possible, Eastern Air Command's VLR Liberators, which proved so vital during the Battle of the Atlantic, were sold for scrap. At the time, there seemed no probability of their being needed again. Fortuitously, the dearth of a suitable long-range maritime aircraft was rectified by refurbishing many of the Mark X Lancasters still in storage on the prairies. Ironically, to fulfill this need some Lancasters had to be repurchased from scrap dealers.

Technology after WW II made the MR Lancaster obsolete as an effective ASW aircraft. Something new was needed (1950)

Photo: DND

[3] Canada was responsible for over one million square miles of ocean bounded by 40-60 N latitudes and 35-66 W longitudes.

Sixty Lancasters were converted to the Maritime Reconnaissance (MR) role to work cooperatively with the Royal Canadian Navy (RCN) and other allied forces. Maritime Group began training in all aspects of maritime operations, including: reconnaissance, visual and radar search, shadowing, illuminating, convoy escort, electronic counter measures and strikes against submarines and surface units at sea and in harbour. The techniques for detecting and attacking submarines had progressed little since the end of the Second World War with the visual search still being the primary sensor. The X-band APS-33 radar offered only marginal improvement over its Second World War H2S predecessor for detecting submarines at night or in reduced visibility. When a target was detected on radar, the Lancaster would turn to attack with depth charges before the target submerged. If the submarine dove before the aircraft arrived on top, the navigator dropped a circular pattern of sonobuoys around the radar datum. Two sonobuoy operators aurally monitored the sonobuoys using comparative submarine noise strength to localize the target with sufficient accuracy to attack with homing torpedoes. A successful blind attack[4] depended on the crew's aural acuity.

Photo: DND
Painting: Rob Arsenault

Even though the MR Lancasters had been almost new when taken on strength in the late 1940's, they were quickly becoming obsolete; wiring and electronics were problematic and spares were difficult to procure. More importantly, they could no longer keep up with modern, more sophisticated submarines as effectively as could the newer British Avro Shackleton or the American Lockheed P2V Neptune maritime patrol aircraft.

As early as 1948, Canadair Limited, located in Montreal made overtures to the RCAF to replace its aging Lancasters with a long-range maritime patrol aircraft. Canadair predicted that the RCAF would need an aircraft capable of patrolling for eight hours, 1,600 km (1,000 miles) from base, at a height of 60 meters (200 feet) and at a speed of 266 km/h (165 mph). The range and endurance estimates were based on a requirement to eliminate any gap in the North Atlantic that would be beyond the range of land-based air patrols. Canadair submitted a proposal to

Canadair original design for a Lancaster replacement was based on the Douglas DC-6

Photo: DND

---

[4] An attack on a submerged submarine with no visual references.

CP-127 Neptune was originally procured as a stop-gap measure to replace the old Lancaster ASW until the new CL-28 Argus could be ready for operation. The Neptune served much longer than originally planned.

Photo: DND

the RCAF for a stretched version of its very successful North Star four-engine transport with either the Wright R-3350, Bristol Hercules or Bristol Centaurus piston engines.

In late 1949, the RCAF issued preliminary operational requirements[5] for a general reconnaissance landplane. The idea being to establish a baseline design against which the candidate aircraft could be compared. The RCAF requested Canadair to produce a preliminary design based on the Douglas DC-6 series of aircraft. Canadair responded with a minimum-cost design concept incorporating the DC-6's wings, power plants, main undercarriage and tail surfaces with a new fuselage and nose gear. The new design resembled a large, unpressurized, tricycle undercarriage Lancaster powered by Wright R-3350 piston engines.

Realizing from the outset that an aircraft based on DC-6 components could not meet all of its requirements; the RCAF conducted a survey of other possible candidates. The British Bristol 175 (Britannia airliner) looked promising but further detailed study would be required. In early 1952, the RCAF contracted Canadair to conduct a study to determine if the Bristol 175, which was scheduled to first fly in the summer of 1952, could meet its general reconnaissance landplane requirements. The study was also to compare the Bristol 175's performance against other aircraft types and assess various engine options. During the investigative period, the RCAF issued a more refined operational requirement,[6] which was valid only until 1952. The new requirement specified the aircraft's performance, crew accommodation, equipment and additional features. The requirement called for an aircraft with a greater payload, interior room and comfort than the previous Canadair submission. Curiously, the armament requirement called for the aircraft to carry sonobuoys and bombs; but no mention is made of homing torpedoes, which were the most advanced weapon against submarines during the Second World War.

[5] Operational Requirement No. OR.II/L-10, dated 10 December 1949
[6] Operational Requirement No. OR/10, General Reconnaissance Landplane, undated, but valid until only 1952.

PUTTING *MEANING* INTO DEFENCE

A new dimension of sea safety

The Canadair CL-28 is the most formidable search, strike and kill maritime patrol weapon in the air today. It is in quantity production for the Royal Canadian Air Force and is available for purchase.

The CL-28—a direct derivative of the Bristol Britannia— carries the most comprehensive collection of electronic and other detection equipment ever assembled into one aircraft for locating, tracking and 'fixing' enemy submarines— whether submerged, 'snorting', or on the surface. Once contact is made, torpedoes, depth bombs and other offensive weapons are released.

It was specifically designed for long periods of ocean patrol duty . . . tactical coordination with naval surface craft on defensive and offensive manoeuvres . . . convoy and search-rescue operations.

The CL-28 will meet or surpass the requirements of friendly countries responsible for the defence of coastlines and sea approaches. For full information, write directly to vice-president/sales.

CANADAIR
LIMITED, MONTREAL

- Aircraft   • Research and Development
- Guided Missiles   • Nuclear Engineering

CA57-CANT-1R

SERVING CANADA'S FUTURE...TODAY

More than one thousand miles from base, the giant Argus "sub-killer" and its crew of specialists, vigilantly patrol the seas. The most advanced electronic detection equipment aids them in their vital work. This is an around-the-clock patrol for Canada and NATO, by the men and aircraft of the RCAF Maritime Air Command.

These specially trained aircrew members and their ground support teams are deft and capable. Their aircraft and detection equipment are unsurpassed in Maritime operations.

Ask your local RCAF Career Counsellor how you can serve Canada today as an aircrew or ground team member of the Air Force.

AF-60-1M

ROYAL CANADIAN AIR FORCE

The RCAF specification issued on 21 July, 1952, called for a maritime reconnaissance landplane developed from the Bristol Britannia (Bristol 175)

Photo: BOAC

In May 1952, the evaluation of the Bristol 175 was far from complete. However, Air Marshall Curtis, Chief of the Air Staff, realized that if the new aircraft was to be delivered with minimum delay, the approval process must be started as soon as practicable. Curtis, therefore, requested authority[1] from the Minister of National Defence to proceed with the development of a prototype of the maritime version of the Bristol 175 aircraft. Curtis explained that the Lancaster would be viable only until 1955 and proposed to introduce the Lockheed P2V-6 Neptune to fill the gap created by the Lancaster's predicted early obsolescence and the entry of a new maritime aircraft into service. The Air Marshal emphasized that an aircraft with greater range and endurance than any aircraft currently flying or in production was required to close the mid-Atlantic gap and that after a number of design studies, the RCAF favoured the Bristol 175. The Bristol design was not only adaptable to the maritime role but its performance, compared to the Lancaster, would also require fewer numbers to provide a force of equivalent flying capability. Additionally, it had the advantage that the same basic aircraft could be used as a heavy transport replacement for the RCAF's North Stars, and that Trans

RCAF Specification Air 15-11 issued on 21 July 1952, called for a maritime reconnaissance landplane developed from the Bristol Britannia (Bristol 175). The CL-28 is born (1952).

Photo: Mike Vacheresse

[1] Secret Memorandum S60-3-95 (DAO), dated 27 May 1952

Canada Airlines was interested in a turbo-prop version of the aircraft on its North Atlantic routes. Curtis suggested that these possible uses might result in a large enough order to justify manufacture in Canada.

Curtis reported that Bristol ascertained that the cost of the bare airframe in the U.K. was approximately $846,000, not including profit or development charges levied by the Ministry of Supply. At the time, Bristol was tooled for a total production run of 25 aircraft. If Canadian production was tooled for a total of 60 to 80 aircraft, the resultant efficiency might more than offset an increased Canadian cost due to higher labour rates. There were two candidate power plants for the aircraft, the Napier Nomad compound diesel which was under development and therefore, no costs were available and the Wright R-3350 turbo-compound at $80,000 each or $320,000 per aircraft.

Engineers conduct ditching tests on CL-28 Argus test models (Canadair 1955)
Photo: Greenwood Aviation Museum Collection

The authorization to proceed with development of a prototype of the maritime version of the Bristol 175 was contingent upon RCAF satisfaction with the flying characteristics of the commercial version following flight trials in June/July (1952).

In lieu of Bristol producing the complete prototype aircraft it was recommended that all parts common to both the commercial and maritime version be purchased, i.e. wings, tailplane, rudder, undercarriage, etc and that the manufacturing of the fuselage be completed in Canada. This course of action had the advantage that if subsequent production in Canada were to follow, most of the fuselage tooling would already be in place. The disadvantage was that extensive liaison would be required between Bristol and a Canadian manufacturer.

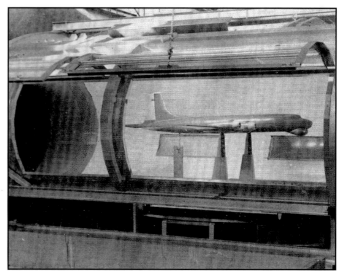

The Air Marshall estimated the prototype would not be able to fly before the spring of 1954 and that the following evaluation period was expected to last until the fall of 1954. If the evaluation proved successful, Curtis advised the RCAF would request authorization for full production, resulting in the first aircraft being available to the RCAF in the spring

Wind tunnel testing of the CL-28 (Canadair 1955)
Photo: Greenwood Aviation Museum Collection

of 1956. An annual production rate of 12 to 18 aircraft per year would require funds in the order of $22-33 million per year. Air Marshall Curtis concluded the memorandum by recommending authorization to proceed with development of the prototype aircraft. In terms of today's fiscal

Curtis summarized estimated production costs per aircraft:

Airframe (including profit and Canadian manufacture)	$1,250,000
Power Plants	$ 320,000
Armament, Electronics	$ 300,000
	$1,870,000

2011 climate, that would equate to just under $15 million dollars per aircraft.

Meanwhile, on the 17th of June 1952, Air Vice Marshall D.M. Smith, Air Member for Technical Services, convened a meeting to plan the conversion the Bristol 175 to a maritime aircraft reconnaissance aircraft to meet RCAF requirements. The plan called for:[2]

- The RCAF to conduct a flight evaluation on the prototype Bristol Britannia airliner in October 1952;
- An Operational Requirement to be completed by 15 July 1952 and be the basis for an Air Specification;
- Canadair to design a new maritime reconnaissance fuselage and build a fuselage mockup;
- The Wright R-3350 engines to be installed;
- Canadair to be ultimately responsible for all engineering;
- Although flight evaluation had not yet been completed, a Contract Demand to fund an engineering study to be let immediately;
- All aircraft to be built in Canada;
- Prototype aircraft to be built using components supplied from Bristol;
- All production aircraft to be re-engineered to use American standard parts;
- Although the RCAF's immediate interest was in the maritime reconnaissance configuration, it was acknowledged that there was interest in a military and commercial transport aircraft; and;
- Prototype and production costs and schedules to be determined.

Testing the Wright R-3350 turbo-compound piston engine (Canadair 1956)

Photo: Greenwood Aviation Museum Collection

Two days later on 20 June 1952, Air Marshall Curtis advised the Minister of National Defence that the RCAF,

[2] File: 1038-Bristol 175, Minutes of Meeting held at AFHQ, 17 June 1952

CL-28 No. 20710 takes to the air on a test fight
Photo from: DND

Canadair and Bristol had agreed on preliminary arrangements to produce the prototype.[3] Curtis assured the Minister that he had secured agreement from Mr. C.D. Howe, the Deputy Minister for Munitions and Supply, to build a prototype in Canada. This was a politically astute move as, in the aviation industry, Mr. Howe was unofficially known as the "Deputy Minister for Everything" and nothing happened in defence circles without his concurrence. Curtis further advised the Minister that he would inform Mr. Howe when estimated costs and a method of proceeding with the project were finalized.

On 8 July 1952, the Cabinet approved the Minister of Department of National Defence's recommendation that funds be made available to enable one Bristol 175 to be secured and tested for suitability as a maritime aircraft with a view to undertake full production in 1955-56.[4]

Anticipating that production of the prototype maritime version of the

Canadair Argus CL-28, VN710 sports her new lightning bolts (1957)
Photo: DND

[3] Memorandum from W.A. Curtis to Minister, dated 20 June 1952
[4] Letter from Cabinet Secretary to CAS, Re: Cabinet Conclusions for 8 July, dated 18 July 1952

Bristol 175 would be approved, the RCAF had already prepared Specification Air 15-11, which provided specifications for an aircraft that would meet its operational requirements.

The specification issued on 21 July 1952, called for a maritime reconnaissance landplane developed from the Bristol Britannia (Bristol 175) with greater payload, interior space and comfort than Canadair's earlier North Star proposal and powered by four Wright R-3350-85 engines.

Photo: DND

The main role of the aircraft was the protection of the sea lines of communication and had to be capable of performing the following tasks:

- Search, shadow and attack enemy submarines;
- Search, shadow and attack enemy surface vessels;
- Mine laying; and
- Search and Rescue operations.

The bomb bay had to be capable of carrying:

- Four active homing torpedoes or four passive homing torpedoes;
- Twelve depth bombs or six 500 lb bombs;
- Ten mines (1000 lb each), or twenty-four 500 lb bombs; or
- Thirty-two practice bombs, or four photo-flash bombs.

In late 1952, the reconnaissance landplane program achieved a major milestone when Air Marshall Curtis advised the Minister that the engineering study and flight trials with the Bristol 175 had been completed with the conclusion that;[5] "the Bristol 175 will make a very satisfactory replacement for the Lancaster in the maritime role; and the aircraft will also make a suitable replacement for the North Star

Photo: DND

[5] Memorandum From W.A. Curtis to The Minister, dated 3 December 1952
[6] This conclusion portended the production of the CC-106 Yukon transport for the RCAF and its civilian version the CL-44.

A beautiful shot of No. 20714 on a test flight

Photo:DND

as a heavy military transport." [6]

In accordance with the Cabinet caveat, that approval for the maritime prototype production was contingent upon a successful completion of the Bristol 175 flight trials. Curtis requested authorization to proceed with construction of the prototype. He confirmed the RCAF's intention to have Bristol build the components that were common to civil and military versions of the aircraft and those parts that were not common to the civil transport, i.e. nose turret, tail turret, bomb-bays, etc be manufactured by Canadair.[7] Estimated costs for the prototype were $11,131,000. If the decision was made to go into production the estimated cost per aircraft was $2,834,241. Based a production run of 54 aircraft, the cost of the program would be $164,180,014.

On January 23rd 1953, the Department of Defence Production (DDP) advised Air Vice Marshall Smith that licensing discussions were underway between Bristol and Canadair and requested the RCAF to state the number of aircraft required.[8] Interestingly, DDP appeared unaware of the Bristol 175's search speed and endurance inadequacies and questioned why the Bristol 175 itself could not be used in the maritime reconnaissance role. DDP also questioned why other aircraft had not been evaluated, when, in fact, a Lockheed California proposal with a version of its four-engine Constellation airliner

Photo: DND

---

[7] In this early stage of development the RCAF still had a Second World War perception of ASW and believed that maritime aircraft would require turrets for self-defence.
[8] DDP Letter, File No. B69-12-30, dated 23 January 1953

No. 20715 is prepared for operational evaluation under Maritime patrol conditions (1957)

Photo: DND

was rejected because of its inability to maneuver safely at low airspeeds and low altitudes. A proposal from Douglas Aircraft, based on the DC-7 transport was similarly rejected.

On 7 February 1953, the Deputy Minister National Defence, C. M. Drury, responded to the Department of Defence Production regretting that fleet size numbers could not be provided at this time.[9] But, reaffirmed the need to replace the Lancaster at a rate of 12-15 aircraft per year in peacetime and at considerably higher rates in wartime.[10] He added that there were no immediate plans to replace the North Star with the Bristol 175 and that there would be no difficulty in providing government furnished equipment for the prototype aircraft. Drury rejected the recommendation for two prototype aircraft, acknowledging that the single prototype would not be a complete engineering prototype. However, it would allow the RCAF to establish the suitability of the aircraft for the maritime role. In mid 1953, a joint RCAF/Canadair team visited the Bristol aircraft company in England to evaluate the Britannia as a suitable platform from which to develop a maritime patrol/ASW aircraft. The only concern was the ability of the Britannia's ailerons to provide essential maneuverability in the roll axis at low air speeds. The team decided that this concern could be alleviated by the addition of spoilers to augment roll control.[11]

CL-28 Argus 716, 710 and 713 on Greenwood's flight apron (1957)

Photo: DND

---

[9] Secret Deputy Minister Letter, S1038-109, dated 7 February 1953
[10] RCAF plans had to consider the possibility of Cold War hostilities breaking out before the production of the maritime version was completed.
[11] On the Britannia the pilot's control wheel was linked to trim tabs on the trailing edges of the ailerons, vice the actual ailerons, as was the usual practice.

Photo: DND

> The Contract schedule called for delivery of the:
>
> - First pre-production CL-28 in November 1956,
> - First production CL-28 in February 1957,
> - Second production CL-28 in April 1957, and
> - The remainder at a rate of one per month.

In late 1953, Cabinet Defence Committee Document D 50/53, dated 26 November 1953, was prepared for Cabinet approval to procure a maritime version of the Bristol 175. Admiral W.B. Creary RCN, Chief of Naval Staff, supported forwarding the document to Cabinet with the proviso that 1954-55 funding estimates be limited to the production of a flying prototype.[12] Admiral Creary's recommendation was based on a joint RCN/RCAF Sea/Air Warfare Committee report on the suitability of the RCAF's proposed acquisition of 50 Bristol 175 and 25 Lockheed Neptune P2V-7 ASW aircraft.
The committee opined that:

- There was a requirement to replace the Lancaster aircraft for the RCAF squadrons allocated to the Supreme Allied Commander Atlantic (SACLANT);[13]
- Acquisition of the Neptune aircraft as proposed was agreed upon;
- Very Long Range aircraft operating in the mid-Atlantic had a decided advantage over lesser range shore based aircraft in ability to remain on patrol over the convoy;
- SACLANT estimated that by 1956 anti-submarine weapons will have progressed to the stage where their operational use is practical and may affect his 1956 Force Requirements;
- Neither the United States nor the British are embarking on a long-range patrol aircraft such as the Bristol 175;
- Current aircraft such as the Shackleton and P2V Neptune are approaching their maximum equipment and weapon capacity;

RAF Shackleton

Photo:DND

---

[12] Secret Chairman, Chiefs of Staff letter, dated 3 December 1953
[13] In the event of hostilities, operational control of 404 and 405 Squadrons would be transferred from the RCAF to SACLANT. Similarly, when 415 Squadron was reactivated it also would be transferred to SACLANT"s operational control.

A polished new CP-107 Argus MK I is handed over to the RCAF's Maritime Air Command (Greenwood, 1958)

Photo from: DND

The second Argus Aircraft was delivered in bare metal with very austere markings and without the fuselage flash and carried the 404 "Buffalo "Squadron's SP unit code.

Profile Drawing: Rob Aresenault

There was some doubt about the effectiveness of very long range aircraft as an anti-submarine weapon because of its limited maneuverability and inability to detect submerged submarines; and there was a need for scientific evaluation of future overall anti-submarine policy.

Admiral Creary was particularly interested in the report's final recommendation. To confirm that long-range aircraft would complement other ASW initiatives,[14] he requested a scientific evaluation of future Canadian ASW policy, both surface and air, be completed before approval was granted for full production of the Bristol 175 ASW aircraft.

---

14 The RCN was in the process of acquiring the aircraft carrier, HMCS Bonaventure, 100 carrier borne CS2F Tracker ASW aircraft and a new ASW helicopter.

The first Argus, No. 20710 rolls off the production line on the 21st of December, 1956

Photo: DND

The committee's recommendations reinforced the RCAF's need to replace the Lancaster with the interesting comment that SACLANT foresaw the increased capability of the maritime version of the Bristol 175 reducing his force requirements. It is ironic that the committee had doubts about the effectiveness of a large aircraft when it is considered that the largest VLR aircraft in the Second World War, the B-24 Liberator, was the allies' most successful ASW vehicle, credited with 72 U-boats destroyed. Similarly, the committee omitted any mention of submarine acoustic detection systems, which, although in their infancy, had proved to have a promising future in ASW during the Second World War.

By the end of 1953, the RCAF had satisfied Cabinet that the Britannia could meet all of its requirements and on 23 February 1954 the government announced that Canadair would build the new aircraft based on the Britannia. On 16 March, the license agreement with Bristol was signed and on 27 May, Canadair was awarded a contract to produce an initial 13 maritime patrol/ASW aircraft, designated the CL-28.

The CL-28 prototype (No. 20710) rolled off the production line 21 December 1956 and shortly thereafter, on 5 February 1957, the RCAF named the CL-28 the "Argus". There are at least six Argus's in Greek mythology, but in the spirit of its seeing-all surveillance role, the CL-28 was named for Argus Panoptes, the monster with 100 eyes, only two of which would close at any one time. After ground testing, No. 20710 made its first flight on 28 March 1957 and along with the following five, the production Argus entered a prolonged flight test program. Argus No. 20710[15] was used for stability and control testing; 20711 for systems and environmental testing; 20712 for cold weather trials; 20713 for structural integrity and RCAF performance handling; 20714 for weapons evaluation; 20715 for operational evaluation under maritime patrol conditions.[16]

---

[15] The engineering development Argus, unofficially numbered 20709, became the Flight Procedures Trainer and the Tactical Crew Procedures Trainer, i.e. simulators, at RCAF Station Greenwood.
[16] After integration of Canada's armed services in 1968, the Argus CL-28 nomenclature was changed to CP-107. Argus serial numbers were changed to begin with 107 so that the former 20710 became 10710 etc.

Passing the maritime torch. 25 Lockheed P2V-7 Neptunes were purchased to fill the gap created by the Lancaster's predicted early obsolescence and the entry of the new Argus Maritime aircraft into service.

Photo: DND

The Lancaster was quickly becoming obsolete and difficult to maintain; it would not be capable of meeting the increasing Soviet maritime threat until the last of the Argus were delivered. Therefore, as originally proposed by the RCAF, and supported by the Navy, an interim maritime patrol aircraft was required to fill the void. In late 1954, the RCAF placed an order for 25 Lockheed P2V-7 Neptune maritime patrol aircraft directly off the production line. The Neptune was a proven design in use with the U.S. Navy; all 25 were delivered in less than six months to bridge the gap between the Lancaster and the still-on-the-drawing-board Argus.

Before the completion of the first batch of Argus aircraft, Canadair received a contract for twenty additional slightly modified versions designated the Argus Mark 2. The principal difference being that the American APS-20 air search radar used in the first thirteen Argus Mark 1's was replaced with the British Air-to-Surface-Vessel (ASV) 21 radar, which was specifically designed for maritime surface search. With the first six Argus's coming off the production line being used for flight-testing, the first operational Argus was not officially turned over to Maritime Air Command until May 17, 1958 at RCAF Station Greenwood. With 33 Argus and 25 Neptunes the RCAF had a total of 58 maritime patrol aircraft, 17 fewer aircraft than the originally planned total of 75 Argus and Neptunes. As with many Canadian interim measures, the Neptune remained in service until 1968, much longer than originally planned.

Development of the Argus was a tremendous challenge for Canadair. The task of converting a fast, pressurized, high-flying airliner into a low and slow flying, unpressurized, piston engine patrol plane loaded with tons of sophisticated electronic equipment and weapons was enough to deter even the most experienced engineers. As planned, Canadair retained the Britannia's wings, tail and flight control system, but had to design a completely new fuselage with two massive 5.5 meter (18 feet) weapons bays that could accommodate up 3,600 kg (8,000 lbs) of torpedoes, bombs, depth charges or mines. A 70-million candlepower high intensity searchlight was mounted on the starboard wing for target

Wright R-3350 turbo-compound piston engine was the only piston engine where the 3,700-horse power produced exceeded the 3,350 cubic inch displacement of the 18 cylinders

Photo: Tom Gosling

identification at night. A redesigned nose with a transparent observer's position, a new landing gear to accommodate a large chin radome and the addition of a 5.59-meter (18 feet) tail boom to isolate the magnetic anomaly detection sensor from the aircraft's magnetism gave the Argus a distinctive silhouette.

The Britannia's four Proteus turboprop engines were not ideal for low altitude operations and as a result they were replaced with Wright R-3350 turbo-compound piston engines. The R-3350's represented the maximum design limits for piston engines and provided a combination of high power and low fuel consumption. In fact, it was the only piston engine where the 3,700-horse power produced exceeded the 3,350 cubic inch displacement of the 18 cylinders. To withstand the beating it would take in a turbulent wave-top environment, the airframe required considerable strengthening. As a result, the Argus established many Canadian manufacturing firsts; it became the first Canadian design to make extensive use of metal-to-metal bonding, and the first wide use in Canada of titanium and high strength aluminum alloy. Another Canadian first was the isolation of the top of the vertical fin with a structural plastic material, thereby allowing the fin cap to be used as an antenna. Despite serious doubts from aircraft manufacturing giants such as Boeing, Canadair became the world's first manufacturer to parallel and synchrophase four 400-cycle generators to meet the Argus's huge AC electrical requirements for its latest state-of-the-art avionics and ASW systems. Another monumental task was the conversion of over 9,000 Bristol engineering drawings to North American standards.

Extensive wind tunnel tests were carried out at National Aeronautical Establishment, Ottawa. These tests were directed mainly toward determining the effect on drag and other aerodynamic characteristics of the power plants and the various protuberances; developing the wing spoiler system referred to previously; and determining the dropping characteristics of various stores and items of equipment. A full-scale structural test of the fuselage was carried out. Because of the size of the fuselage a

Photo: DND

Four Wright R-3350 turbo-compound engines provided the Argus with just over 14,000 lbs of horse power
Photo: DND

Ab Initio Argus aircrew training occurred at RCAF Station Greenwood with the Argus Conversion Unit (ACU). Argus Mk 1 20718 was assigned to this unit. Note the higher than normal ensign placement on the vertical tail of 718. This aircraft also later served with 415 "Swordfish" Squadron until the late 1960's. CAF unification brought 718 a "posting" to 407 "Demon" Squadron in CFB Comox where she finished off her career. This aircraft was dispatched to Burbank California in March of 1979 to greet her replacement—the CP-140 "Aurora".

Profile Drawing: Rob Arsenault

special rig had to be built, consisting of an immense structural steel platform on which the fuselage was mounted; the loads being applied through a system of hydraulic jacks.

The Argus had an innovative crew layout, which incorporated an entirely new flight deck into the forward fuselage to accommodate two pilots and a flight engineer. Positions for the "Routine" or position keeping navigator and the radio officer responsible for long-range communications were located immediately behind the flight deck. The five basic flight crewmembers grouped in the forward fuselage enabled the Argus to be operated similar to transport aircraft during non-tactical phases of the mission, e.g. transits to and from the search area. The tactical compartment located in the middle of the fuselage was manned by the "Tactical" navigator and five ASW sensor operators. The Argus was the first maritime patrol aircraft to group the tactical crew together to facilitate exchange of tactical information. The tactical navigator was responsible for correlating all sensor information and directing the entire crew through search and localization tactics and the final blind attack.

The Argus had exceptional endurance, setting a record of 30 hours 20 minutes, however, typical maritime patrols varied between 14 and 18 hours duration. When it is considered that the crew started a mission by briefing and planning two hours before take-off and finished debriefing two hours after landing, the crew day easily extended to 22 hours. It was not uncommon for the same ground crew that helped to launch Argus to greet the aircraft on its return 18

734 Flying over the city of Halifax

Photo:DND

hours later however, in the intervening time the ground crew had had the luxury of going home for a night's sleep.

Photo: DND

"Almost two million engineering man-hours logged on the largest aircraft ever produced in Canada."

The adaptation of the Britannia to what became known as the CP-107 Argus resulted in one of the largest engineering design and development programs ever undertaken in Canada. While the original designs of the Britannia were used as much as possible, engineers and technicians expended approximately one and three quarter million man-hours in order to redesign and modify the majority of components and materials for the original Britannia design. Additionally, in order to ensure future logistic and maintenance support in time of emergency, all aspects of the design process had to be "Canadianized" so as to cater for the use of North American materials, hardware and shop procedures. The Bristol design was scrutinized by Canadair and a series of material strength equivalents were determined, selected and compiled as a conversion manual. Furthermore, a systematic procedure for "Canadianization" was developed which allowed a relatively small group of engineers and draftsmen to convert a large number of drawings at a very early stage of the program with great benefit to manufacturing operations. In all, roughly 7,000 wing, tail, flight controls and other drawings were "Canadianized" in this fashion.

Argus MkII 20733 circa 1966 resplendent in 415 "Swordfish" Squadron markings over the new stylized Maple Leaf flag design. 415 Squadron was the first Squadron to display content from the Heraldic Crest on the vertical tail. Re-formed at RCAF Station Summerside in 1961, 415 wasted no time in applying a Dayglow Red-Orange 'Sydney' Swordfish to the tail of their aircraft. A photo of 733 in this paint scheme was featured in the Journal-Pioneer newspaper ad for in every one of Summerside's Air Force Day Open House flyers. It is Rob's favourite.
Profile Drawing: Rob Arsenault

Practice makes perfect. Maritime Air Command crews worked with RCN submarines to hone their sub hunting and killing skills. When introduced into service, the Argus was the most advanced ASW or Maritime Reconnaissance (MR) aircraft in operation (1962).

The Argus's sophisticated navigation and sensor systems coupled with its long range and endurance made it NATO's most effective submarine hunter in the late 1950's and throughout the 1960's. It would be many years before any ASW aircraft would appear to challenge its capabilities. In addition to the APS-20 and ASV 21 radars, the Argus's repertoire of leading state-of-the-art ASW sensors included Magnetic Anomaly Detection (MAD) to accurately pin point a submerged submarine's position. It did this by detecting the distortion it created in the earth's magnetic field. Electronic Support Measures (ESM) were used to detect and identify submarine radar transmissions, Exhaust Trail Indicator (ETI) to detect a submarine's diesel engine emissions, and Explosive Echo Ranging (EER), which employed active sonar principles to detect submerged submarines.[1]

Search Radar

The Argus had two different radar systems. The AN/APS 20 radar was an airborne, high powered, "S" band search radar, originally designed as part of an Airborne Early Warning (AEW) system. It was capable of searching to a range of 200 nautical miles at an altitude of 25,000 feet and to 100 nautical miles at 5,000 feet. It was employed in the Mark 1 Argus as an ASW radar.

Due to the high power of this radar, sea clutter was a major factor in short range target discrimination and it was almost ineffective for detection purposes in sea state over 3 (wave heights 2–3.5 feet). The first 13 Argus had the APS-20 radar installed and were easily identified by the large chin mounted radar dome located at the front of the aircraft.

Radome on the MK 1 Argus for the APS 20

Photo: DND

AN/APS 20 radar station inside the Argus Mk I

Photo: DND

[1] Explosive charges were dropped adjacent to a sonobuoy; the radiated sound reflected from the submarine (echo) was detected by the sonobuoy and produced an accurate range of the target from the sonobuoy.

Flight engineer station and cockpit

The ASV-21 radar was a medium powered "X" band search radar specifically designed for operations against small targets such as submarine snorkels and periscopes. The term "ASV" is an abbreviation for Anti-Surface Vessel and this radar was the latest of a long series of ASV radars. The series began early in WW II and was upgraded with improvements to meet the improved capability of the submarine which was the principle target of the ASV-21 radar. This radar was primarily used in the Royal Air Force Shackleton and the Mark II Argus. The last 20 Argus built had the ASV-21 installed and could the identified by the small chin mounted radar dome located at the front of the aircraft.

ASV-21 radar was the primary search radar employed on the Argus MkII
Photo: DND

Mcpl Brian Chipman, an observer with 415 Squadron, Radar Fixing on the ASV 21 Radar.
Photo: DND

Low Frequency Analyzer and Recorder — JEZEBEL

Low Frequency Analyzer and Recorder (LOFAR) system, referred to as Jezebel to cloak its true function, was the most effective submarine detection sensor. Similar to the earlier VLR Liberators and Lancasters, the Argus dropped patterns of multiple sonobuoys in a submarine search area and passively listened for the low frequency sounds produced by a submarine's propeller, diesel engines or turbines. The detected sounds were transmitted from the sonobuoy to the Argus via one of 31 VHF radio channels assigned to each sonobuoy. But, instead of crewmembers aurally estimating strengths of submarine sounds, as was done in earlier aircraft, Jezebel provided a much more scientific approach. Jezebel not only computed the relative strengths of the submarine sounds detected by the sonobuoy, but also displayed the frequencies of the sounds that uniquely identified or fingerprinted each class of submarine. The Jezebel system had the advantage of searching a wide area while the passive listening nature of the sonobuoys avoided alerting the submarine that was being hunted. Throughout Argus service, the Jezebel system was upgraded only once, however, significant gains were made in the design of sonobuoys to keep pace with the ever-quieter submarines. The continual redesign of sonobuoy hydrophones improved their sensitivity and hydrophone suspension system improvements reduced ambient ocean noise, thereby increasing the ability to detect quieter submarines at longer ranges.[2] Also, the option to select deeper hydrophone depths permitted the sonobuoy to listen at the deeper diving depths of the newer submarines. Variable sonobuoy life selections

---

[2] Hydrophones were suspended by a cable up to 300 meters below the surface float that transmitted submarine sounds to the aircraft. A bungee cord type segment of the suspension cable reduced hydrophone bobbing and hence flow noise caused by wave motion and currents.

(30 min, 1 hour, and 8 hours) provided tactical flexibility; the longer lives catered to long term area surveillance operations while the shorter life sonobuoys were tailored to track faster evading submarines that quickly outpaced a sonobuoy's detection range. The variable sonobuoy life selection was essential to avoid congestion of the relatively few 31 VHF sonobuoy channels.

Jezebel also provided a bearing of the target from a sonobuoy using a technique called Correlated Detection and Recording (CODAR). Using the ANTAC system, the tactical navigator dropped two sonobuoys 2000 meters apart thereby providing a baseline for the Jezebel system to convert the phase difference of the submarine sound arriving at each sonobuoy in a CODAR pair into a bearing. The classical tactical sequence started with Jezebel detecting a submarine signature on one or more sonobuoys in a search pattern, followed by dropping two CODAR sonobuoy pairs to obtain intersecting bearings that indicated the target's position. The position was further refined using EER with the resulting datum being attacked with a pattern of four homing torpedoes. The accuracy of the attack could usually be assessed by the magnitude of the magnetic anomaly detected by MAD.

Explosive Echo Ranging – Julie

Sgt. Ray Allen, Observer with 415 Squadron Summerside, works at the Julie Station

Photo: DND

Julie or Explosive Echo Ranging, was developed by F/L Ted Delong, RCAF, that resulted in a joint development project between the RCAF and the USN (United States Navy). Julie was an active sensor that placed an explosive charge in the water next to a sonobuoy. The sound energy would radiate out in all directions and when the energy hit an object it would bounce back an echo to the sonobuoy. Using a special stop watch the operator would start it when he heard the initial explosion and stop it when he heard an echo. The watch would then show the distance the contact was from the buoy. The Tactical Navigator (TAC-NAV) would then draw a circle equal to the range around the buoy on the tactical plot. In order to establish a position of the contact, other buoys, placed in a geometric pattern, would also have to have contact, thus producing a number of circles that would reduce ambiguity and pin point the contact. Since this was an active method of sub hunting, the submarine knew you were there and what you were doing so he would take evasive action to break away from contact and disappear. The explosive detonations and subsequent contact echo was also displayed on the AJH 501 moving paper display. Special rulers were used to measure ranges. Many operators found that by listening to the raw sounds from the sonobuoy they could increase the range of detection by 20 percent in many cases. Maximum range for Julie detection was about 2000 yards and was dependant on water temperature, depth of the sonobuoy hydrophone, explosive charge and contact.

Julie Stop Watch
Photo: Bert Campbell

An Argus Mk II from 415 sqn searched for Soviet submarines off the coast of Greenland (1970)

Photo: DND

The Magnetic Anomaly Detector (MAD) was an accurate, short range detection system used to detect underwater targets. Anomaly means deviation, irregularity or variation. The magnetic field surrounding the earth is relatively uniform in any given area. The presence of a magnetic body, such as a submarine, causes a distortion of this normally uniform field and the MAD system is employed to detect these magnetic anomalies produced by the presence of a submarine in the earth's magnetic field. The Argus was installed with the ASQ-8 MAD system with the detection head located in the MAD boom that extended out the rear of the aircraft. This was to remove the head as far away as possible from the electrical systems on the aircraft.

Side profile of the MAD Boom with lightning diverter

Profile Drawing: Rob Arsenault

When a submarine contact was obtained by Radar, ECM, Julie, Jezebel or visual sighting, a relatively accurate fix was established. MAD was then employed to confirm the presence of a submarine and, because of the short detection range, further refine the fix. Then once MAD contact has been gained, tracking could be carried out by establishing a course and speed of the submarine with sufficient accuracy for a homing torpedo attack. MAD tracking tactics were also used to track a submarine for extended periods of time should, for example, an aircraft expend all of its weapons and have to wait for relief forces to take over prosecuting the target.

Another tactic was the patrolling of a small strategic area, such as a harbour, that would have been a prime target for a submarine by deploying MAD patrols across the harbour mouth. This was used successfully during WW II in the Gibraltar Barrier.

Electronic Surveillance Measures

The Argus was equipped with an Electronic Surveillance Measures (ESM) suite used to detect submarine and surface ship radars. The suite consisted of an AN/ALR-8 which had intercept and DF functions and the AN/APA-74 for signal pulse analyzing. The antennae for this suite was located in a bubble just forward of the rear bottom access hatch.

When submarines had to recharge their batteries they would come to periscope depth and put up their ESM mast to see if there was any unwelcome radars in the area. Then the periscope was put up to get a quick look around to see if there were any contacts. Finally, their radar mast would be extended and would be on for one 360° sweep to see if there were and contacts around. It was when the one sweep was made that the Argus ESM suite was designed for. When a radar signal was received it would show a bearing to the unknown contact and the radar signal itself could then be analyzed to

ESM operator
Photo: DND

determine what radar they detected. This information was then used to narrow down the possibilities as to the identity of the contact. Submarine radars were unique and therefore not too difficult to identify. The system was also used to detect and track surface ships, especially non-friendly naval ships. Surface ships, however, were another issue as many different platforms used the same radars.

Exhaust Trail Indicator

The exhaust gases given off by internal combustion engines contain a certain amount of extremely small particles of unburned fuel and waste. These particles are left suspended in the air and form trails when carried along by the wind. As the trail gets longer, they get wider, less intense and finally dissipate.

The Submarine Detection Set AN/ASR-3 also known as Exhaust Trail Indicator (ETI) was designed to detect the presence of these particle trails and to analyze the relative particle density in a given air sample. Comparison between the particle densities in a trail and the clear surrounding air plus a measurement of the trail width provided information useful in the detection and localization of the contaminating source. Not all sources were from a submarine, as surface ships and land-based heavy industry also emitted these particles.

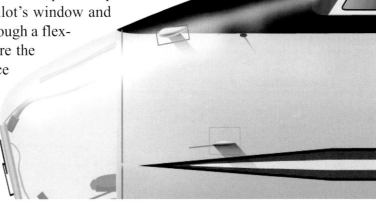

The air samples were collected by an air scoop on the port side of the nose, half way between the pilot's window and nose lookout position, and passed through a flexible tube to the particle detector where the air samples were tested for the presence and concentration of exhaust particles. It then provided an aural and visual signal to the operator, proportional to the particle content. The information was then passed to the TacNav for plotting.

Above: Graphic representation of the ETI Scoop

Profile Drawing: Rob Arsenault

Left: Exhaust Trail Indicator

Photo: DND

33

Visual Detection

Visual or the Mark One Eyeball was another detection method used, especially in the early days when submarines had to put up induction and exhaust masts to recharge their batteries. There were three lookout positions in the aircraft: the nose and the two observation positions at the rear of the aircraft. The pilot and co-pilot positions also offered ideal views. The best seat was the nose position with a clear 180° view of the earth and sky and being forward of the engines the only noise was the air rushing past the aircraft. The three lookout positions were usually manned for one hour at a time to reduce fatigue except for search and rescue missions when 20-minute rotations were used. The two lookout positions in the rear of the aircraft were dual hatted as they were also responsible for releasing the internal search and track stores for the Tac-Nav. Cameras were also available at each lookout position for taking photos.

Cpl. Bill Lukey operates a Hulcher camera equipped with an 11" lens on Argus patrols. Air photographs were taken of every contact.

Photo: DND

A rare "hairy" view from the nose of the Argus. Many a periscope were spotted from this station.

Photo: Leif Wadelius

A night time, aid for visual search was the 70-million candle power search light located on the outer portion of the starboard wing that was controlled by the pilot. This very bright light was used only when approaching an unknown

The Argus was equipped with a 70,000,000 candle power searchlight.

Photo: DND

contact at night that did not have running lights. The introduction of the nuclear submarine limited visual detection opportunities as it could stay submerged for weeks on end. However, visual detection of nuclear submarine periscopes were made when they came close to the surface for communications breaks.

As with any technology, its effectiveness was only made possible by the highly trained and very capable Royal Canadian Air Force and Canadian Armed Forces Argus crews who manned this venerable aircraft throughout her service into the early 1980's.

The million dollar view
Photo: Douglas J. Fisher

Side Looking Radar - SLAR

In the early '70s, a series of projects at the Maritime Proving and Evaluation Unit were planned to gain experience with Remote Sensing Systems. The most extensive system to be examined was an APS-94D Side Looking Radar (SLAR). The SLAR antenna was 24 feet long and due to the number of others sensors to be installed, was decided to assign a second Argus to MP&EU, dedicated to the remote sensing projects. Argus 107 28 was chosen and in the fall of 1971, it was sent to the Aerospace Engineering and Test Establishment (AETE) at Cold Lake Alberta to have the antenna installation designed, installed and flight tested.

APS-94D Side Looking Radar (SLAR) installed on 728 Argus assigned to MP&EU (1975)

Photo: Greenwood Aviation Museum

It was decided to mount the antenna below the rear bomb bay. The hydraulic actuators for the right rear bomb bay door were disconnected from the hydraulic system and the door was locked closed. Two holes were cut in the door and supporting structure for the antenna protruded through the holes and was attached to the weapon mount hard points in the bomb bay. Racks were also installed in the bomb bay to carry the SLAR RF equipment. In January 1972, 10728 deployed to Phoenix, Arizona, for the installation of the remaining SLAR equipment and acceptance testing. While in Phoenix, 10728 was painted with a Road Runner character and nicknamed "SLARGUS" by Motorola.

The APS-94D used film to record the SLAR imagery. A "wet" process was used to develop the film as it ran through the recorder, allowing near real time presentation of the imagery. The APS-94D was originally designed for the Grumman OV-1D Mohawk reconnaissance aircraft and the recorder station was designed to occupy the area in front of the right seat in the OV-1D cockpit. Two of these stations were installed on the port side of the mid rest area of the Argus, in the area normally occupied by a bunk. One station was used with the wet film process and the other was used to expose the film, but it was processed on the ground and produced higher quality images.

The testing of the SLAR performance was carried out in conjunction with Aerospace Engineering Test Establishment (AETE). In particular, the Moving Target Indicator (MTI) mode would produce imagery, which indicated the radial velocity of targets based on doppler shift. This involved having vehicles of various sizes; travelling up and down a runway at various speeds while SLARGUS flew by to determine the resolution and sensitivity of the MTI.

Later in the program, extensive work was done on the SLAR by the Defence Research Establishment Ottawa to improve the performance of the SLAR through enhanced signal processing. As well, the people in the Department of the Environment used SLAR in their studies of ice in the arctic. This resulted in many flights out of Thule, Greenland over the next several years.

Argus 728 with the SLAR antenna below the fuselage prepares to taxi

Photo: DND

The test crew never determined the real cause (possibly the SLAR antenna being a little off the centre line), but 10728 had about +/- one degree of roll oscillation when flying on autopilot. The period was fairly long, but the back and forth rolling caused a venetian blind effect in the SLAR imagery. It was not practical to hand fly the aircraft to the required steadiness for more than one or two minutes, so it was standard practise for both pilots to lean over on the yoke to try to slow the oscillations down even more.

In April 1975, 10728 participated in Exercise AIDJEX, a study of ice dynamics. There was a station on the arctic ice north of Alaska and 10728 flew several missions out of Inuvik, NWT. The ice station had been built with material and personnel flown in by Hercules. 10728 carried out ice profiling flights and general SLAR imaging of the ice station. One of the characteristics of the SLAR imagery is that it is able to see through snow cover and give an accurate image of the ice below. When the SLAR imagery of the ice station was examined, Capt. Reg Thompson commented on how many major cracks there were. About two weeks later, the ice changed rather dynamically and the station broke into several pieces. The station had to be evacuated using Twin Otter aircraft as there wasn't a piece of ice big enough for the Hercules .

1975 MP & EU Argus 728 equipped with the APS-94D SLAR

Illustration: Rob Arsenault

Another interesting exercise (Exercise Brisk) was conducted in October 1976. Both MP&EU (Maritime Proving and Evaluation Unit) aircraft carried out a rendezvous in the arctic north of Alert, with the RN submarine HMS Sovereign. 10728 was specially equipped with a laser profilometer and carried an infrared line scan camera in addition to the SLAR. 10728 carried out a profiling of the ice surface from the air, while the submarine travelled the same track and profiled the ice from below. Meanwhile, 10729 had been fitted with a new Magnetic Anomaly Detection (MAD) system and laid claim to the most northerly MAD detection of a submarine.

Later in the exercise, 10728 over flew the North Pole to check out how the LTN-51 inertial navigation system and the Marconi OMEGA navigation system performed at the pole. That trip ended with a precautionary engine shut down at about 84N and an uneventful 3-engine landing at Thule. A side bar to the Exercise Brisk saga was the logistic needs of the Argus. Standard fuel for the Argus was 115/145 and it was getting vary scarce. Thule had enough on hand to support one Argus, so 10728 was based in Thule, but the fuel used had to be replaced by the Canadian Forces. 10729 was based in Söndre Strömfjord, Greenland where 115/145 fuel was in good supply. During the next annual exercise to re-supply of the Canadian Forces station at Alert, a Hercules took 115/145 fuel from Söndre Strömfjord to Thule to satisfy the agreement with the USAF.

In August 1977, the SLARGUS era ended when the SLAR was removed from 10728 and the equipment was transferred to the Department of the Environment. It was later installed in a Nordair Lockheed Electra where it continued to be used for ice reconnaissance. 10728 continued with MP&EU until it was retired from service in January 1979.

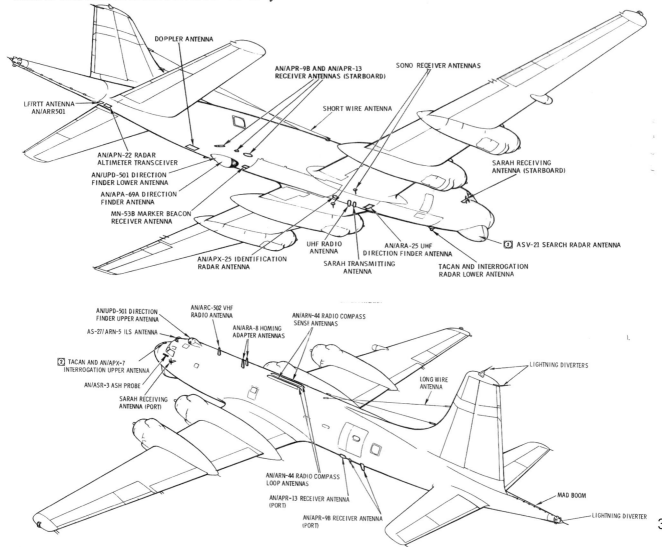

Argus shadow as it flies over a Soviet ice station in the Arctic

Photo: Bert Campbell Collection

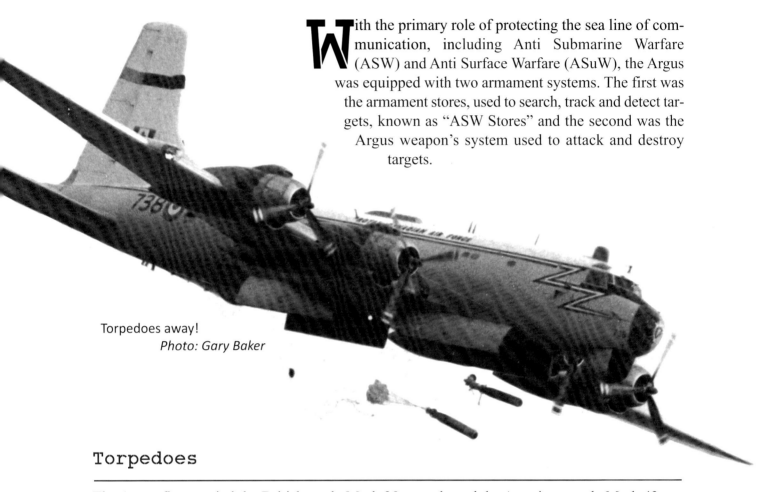

ith the primary role of protecting the sea line of communication, including Anti Submarine Warfare (ASW) and Anti Surface Warfare (ASuW), the Argus was equipped with two armament systems. The first was the armament stores, used to search, track and detect targets, known as "ASW Stores" and the second was the Argus weapon's system used to attack and destroy targets.

Torpedoes away!
Photo: Gary Baker

Torpedoes

The Argus first carried the British made Mark 30 torpedo and the American made Mark 43 torpedo. The Mark 30 was a large eighteen-inch air dropped passive acoustic homing torpedo and was not long in the Argus weapons inventory. The Mk-43 torpedo was the first and smallest of the light-weight anti-submarine torpedoes. This electrically-propelled 10-inch (25-cm) torpedo was 92 inches (2.3 m) long and weighed 265 pounds (120 kg). The torpedo was designed for air or surface launch. The Mod 0 configuration, which was carried by the Argus, was designed for launch from helicopters or fixed-wing aircraft. Electrically driven and deep-diving, this torpedo had a relatively short range. They were classified as obsolete in the 1960's and were replaced by the Mk-44 torpedo.

The Mk-44 was a modular design, consisting of four main sections. The blunt nose contained the active sonar seeker with the 75 pound (34 kg) high explosive warhead immediately behind it. The second section contained the guidance and gyroscopes. The third contained the 24 kilowatt seawater battery which used silver chloride and magnesium electrodes, with seawater acting as the electrolyte. Finally, came the propulsion section, which housed the electric motor, four rectangular control fins and two contra-rotating propellers.

The vacuum tube based guidance system in the Mk-44 was more sophisticated than earlier torpedoes, using pre-launch settings enabling an initial search depth of 50, 150, 250, 450, 650 or

Left to right: LAC C.W Simms, Cpl. S.O Larson and Cpl. J.A McIntosh, M&W Techs at Greenwood, load MK-30 Acoustic Torpedoes into a 405 Squadron Argus.

Photo: DND

900 feet, as well as a search floor at 150, 250, 450, 650 or 900 feet and a maximum dive/climb angle of 4.5, 6 or 7 degrees. On impacting the water, the torpedo either ran out for 1,000 yards or performed a dive at a 30 degree angle to the search depth. After completing this, it performed a flat turn and begun a helical search pattern proceeding up or down until it hit either the minimum depth of 50 yards or the search floor. When it hit either the top or bottom, it performed a flat turn and began to execute the search in reverse. It continued executing this search until it either found a target or exhausted its six minute endurance. The Mk-44 guidance system could drive the active sonar at either a slow rate or a fast rate, which it used when the target drew near to obtain a precise proximity and rate of closure.

The air dropped version of the Mk-44 torpedo was fitted with a parachute retarding system to slow entry into the water, and the nose was pro-

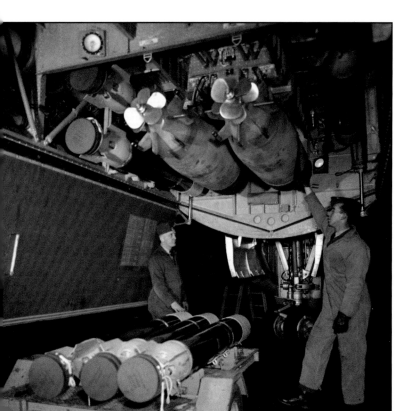

Showing off the size of the Argus weapons capacity as multiple Mk-30 and Mk-43 Torpedoes are loaded in the forward bomb bay.

Photo: DND

tected from the impact by a fairing which was immediately discarded upon entering the water. The propellers were covered by a ring fairing. Shortly after the Mk-44 entered service, it became apparent that newer Soviet submarines were both faster and deeper diving, and could potentially both outrun and out-dive the Mk-44, which was designed to attack targets with a maximum speed of only 17 knots. To address this, an operational requirement was issued that resulted in the acceptance into service of the Mk-46.

The Mk-46 torpedo was designed to attack high performance submarines, and is presently identified as the NATO standard. The Mk-46 was the first American ASW torpedo to utilize a solid-rocket-fueled, hot-gas propulsion system. At four horsepower per pound of engine weight, the Mk-46 torpedo was capable of overtaking the most elusive submarine targets known. It was the first ASW torpedo capable of being launched form a fixed wing aircraft flying at speeds up to 400 knots.

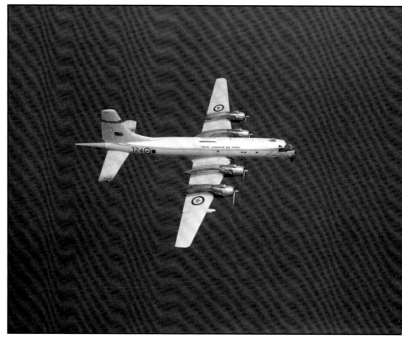

Photo: DND

Mk-54 Depth Bombs

The Mark 54 depth bomb was is in fact a depth charge designed to be dropped from aircraft. A depth bomb had a rather light case. The explosive filler comprised about 70 percent of the weight of the assembled bomb. To reduce the danger of ricochets at small entrance angles, the depth bomb had a flat nose. The tail fuse allowed five choices of depth setting, varying from 25 to 125 feet. Like its close relative the depth charge, a depth bomb was unlikely to hit a submarine directly. Instead, it gained its effect by creating an underwater pressure wave that could weaken or crush the hull plates of the target.

This weapon would normally have been used against conventional submarines that were required to come near the surface to recharge their batteries. The advent of deep diving nuclear submarines reduced its effectiveness significantly.

Mark 46 *Photo: Greenwood Aviation Museum Collection*

Air to air view of the Argus aircraft in flight dropping Depth Charges over the Atlantic ocean.

Photo: DND

Practice Bombs

The Argus had a unique weapons training aid that used to determine attack accuracy. It consisted of a canister carried in the bomb bay that contained up to 12 practice bombs. This was used to simulate depth charge and torpedo attacks.

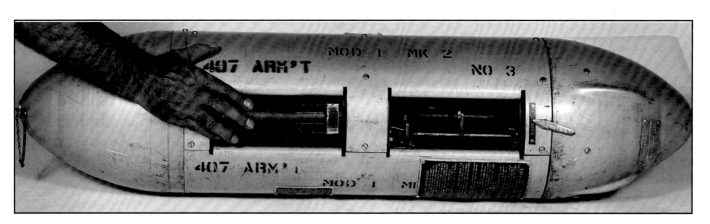

Practice bomb dispenser which expended small practice bombs to simulate attacks

Photo: Greenwood Aviation Museum Collection

Mines and Special Weapons

While the Argus was capable of carrying air-droppable mines, the ability was never developed. As with many older weapon systems, it was felt that if they were needed in the event of a crisis, they could be acquired and trained on quickly. The Argus was also capable of carrying and deploying special Anti-Submarine Weapons, however, official records do not say if any were ever loaded on the Argus.

ASW Stores

Through various ejectors located in the aft portion of the aircraft, the combinations of these stores could be launched from a number of different locations throughout the Argus.

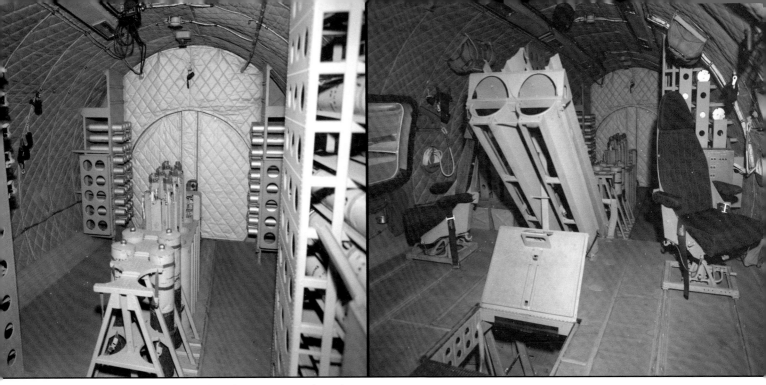

Early ASW stores launch tubes next to the aft lookout positions at the rear of the Argus
Photo: DND

Early ASW stores storage racks and pneumatic sonobuoy launch tubes at the rear of the Argus
Photo: DND

Sonobuoys

Launched from the Argus through various ejectors, located in the aft portion of the aircraft, the ASW Stores consisted of sonobuoys, Signal Underwater Sound (SUS) charges, parachute flares and marine markers. Various combinations of these stores could be launched from a number of different locations throughout the Argus.

Sonobuoys are devices that are launched from aircraft into the water where they deploy a hydrophone to selected depths. The hydrophone picks up the various sounds in the water and transmits them to the aircraft where specialized equipment display the sounds in such a way that trained operators can determine if they are made by natural biological or manmade sources. It is the man made sources that are of interest to the operator who uses both a visual display presentation and aural listening of the sound to determine what is making the sound, be it a submarine or surface ship and can identify the type and nationality of the contact. Since the sonobuoy is passive, the submerged target would not know you were there. Use of a SUS charge dropped near a sonobuoy is called Explosive Echo Ranging and will alert a submarine to your presence and it is used to accurately pinpoint a submerged target to drop a weapon.

Photo: DND

SUS, PDC & Smoke Markers

Signal Underwater Sound (SUS) Charges were used for Explosive Echo Ranging, underwater signalling and to simulate attacks during training exercises. There were two types of SUS charges. The Mark 400 had 1.8 pounds of TNT and the Mark 401 that had 1 ounce of tetryl booster. Both had a length of 15 inches, a diameter of three inches and weighed 6.8 pounds. They also a had two depth settings of either 60 feet or 300 feet. When used with a sonobuoy, they were able to determine the distance from that sonobuoy. When used with a number of sonobuoys, a fairly accurate position of the contact could be determined. For underwater signalling, the number of SUS charges and the time interval between their detonation could be decoded.

Signal Underwater Sound (SUS) Charges were used for Explosive Echo Ranging, underwater signalling
Photo: DND

LUU2/B, Parachute Flare
Photo: Bert Campbell

The parachute flare, LUU2/B, was used to illuminate a large area sufficient enough to permit bombing, reconnoitering or the landing of aircraft. The flare, manufactured by the Thiokol Chemical Corporation, produced an off-white light of approximately 2,000,000 candle power for a duration of approximately five minutes. During the life of the Argus, the parachute flare was used mostly during Search and Rescue operations.

Panier

The panier, though not a weapon, was designed to fit in the forward bomb bay in order to carry cargo such as spare parts and luggage. Designed by Frank Fletcher, at the RCAF #6 Repair Depot, Trenton, Ontario, the project was completed in 1966 and saw the removal of the armament brackets in the forward bomb bay that were replaced with sliding track and panier type trays, which could be removed and pre-loaded before inserted into position. The panier was only used on deployments and the aft bomb bay was still available to carry weapons.

Trailed Weapon Systems

Aerial Rockets

The 2.75-inch diameter folding fin aircraft rocket (FFAR) was an unguided aerial weapon that could be fired from a variety of aircraft in both air-to-air and air-to-ground applications. Unguided air-launched rockets of 2.75 inch diameter were originally developed in the late 1940's to be used by interceptors against heavy bombers. For the Argus, the plan was to use it in the air-to-ground role. The rocket was spin-stabilized and featured four flip-out fins around the nozzle. Maximum range for the 18 pound rocket was around 6,500 yards, but effective range was around 3,700 yards.

2.75-inch diameter folding fin aircraft rocket (FFAR) launcher
Photo: Greenwood Aviation Museum Collection

Argus 718 on the ramp at NAS Corpus Christi Texas with a FFAR pod installed (1958)

Photo: E. J Lewis

The placement of the rocket launch pods between the inboard engines and the fuselage created concerns as the fired rockets did not always fly straight due to some of the folding fins not deploying fully. On one test fire it was reported that a rocket nicked the prop on number 3 engine. Further tests were cancelled and the idea of FFAR for the Argus was shelved.

Bullpup Anti-Surface Missile

In 1960, the RCAF decided to explore options to arm the Argus with anti-shipping or anti-surface missiles. As a result, the first and only to be trailed was the new US AGM-12B Bullpup—an air to surface missile. The Bullpup was designed to be fired from aircraft like the USN A-4 Skyhawk ground attack bombers. In the end, the Bullpup was deemed unsuitable for the Argus, as written in the following story by Argus pilot Dave Wightman:

Stan Waldegger and Dave Wightman were at MPEU Summerside when CEPE Cold Lake undertook the Bullpup trials in Argus 714. Dave was sent from MPEU to be one of the two project pilots, the other being S/L Wilf Speck. The other navigator besides Grant McPhee was Dick Evans and Paul Whitehead was the project test engineer.

All five were on strength of CEPE at the time. Stan was not involved in the trials but may have participated in the analysis of the results later back at MPEU. They deployed 714 from Cold Lake to NAS Point Mugu California, just north of Los Angeles, on 16 Nov 1960, and were there until 24 May 1961, launching about 50 missiles under control of the Pacific Missile Test Range operated by the USN over the ocean. (Including some night launches which were pretty spectacular.)

Argus 714 armed with two AGM12B Bullpup-A anti surface missiles (1960)

Photo: DND

McPhee put everyone to shame in the simulator (an early computer game) as he launched all the missiles and controlled them visually from the nose compartment using a small joystick. The idea was to watch the tracking flares burning at the rear of the missile and keep them superimposed on the target. The missiles were generally launched from as far away as 25,000 feet and from heights of 1500 feet.

The weapon proved not to be suitable for low angle standoff delivery as the slightest error in elevation would cause the missile to hit the water way short or overfly the target and land way long. The Bullpup was designed for high angle launch from fighters and was not suitable for launch from the Argus.

During its time in service, the CP-107 Argus was truly one of the world premier ASW weapons delivery platforms. Her vast array of sensors coupled with her awesome pay load capacity of combined ASW stores and weapons would have caused severe trepidation for any Soviet submarine crew trying to evade her contact. To this day, no other western ASW aircraft has been designed to carry as many weapons as the Argus once could .

Argus 714 Armed with two US AGM-12B Bullpup A during trials (1960)

Profile Drawing: Rob Arsenault

A very rare photo of Argus 714 armed with two AGM-12B Bullpup-A anti surface missiles during trials (1960). Unfortunately the Bullpup was deemed unsuitable for the Argus and no further testing was done to equip the Argus with air to surface anti shipping missiles.

Photo: DND

Lifting the torpedo into the forward bomb bay with an internal winch system made the task quick but no less dangerous

Photo: DND

Photo: DND

Argus 736 of the RCAF in the 60's is being loaded with a full complement of torpedoes prior to an ASW patrol off the East coast.

Photo DND

731 Transits to her patrol area, showing off her clean lines

Photo: DND

The Hunt started with intelligence. Information on where the object of the search was, allowed planners to decide on the geographical area the Argus would be tasked and what methods the aircraft was to use to accomplish their mission. Then a tasking order, known as a Form Green, was issued that directed the base to provide an airborne asset for the mission. A crew and aircraft were then assigned and the preparations began. Based on the Form Green, Argus maintenance personnel would configure the aircraft with appropriate weapons, search stores and fuel. Flight rations were also prepared for the mission.

The crew began their mission planning with an intelligence review to get any updated information that would include a threat assessment, disposition of friendly and unfriendly forces and details on the target of interest. Weather conditions for the mission were studied to determine the appropriate flight profile to, from and while in the patrol area. Oceanographic conditions were briefed that would assist the crew on how best to use the acoustic sensors that provide key information used to plan the mission. That was followed by a crew briefing where the whole mission plan was presented. The last briefing was given prior to entering the patrol area on the tactical plan for the mission.

731 out on patrol decides to have another look at a Soviet fishing trawler that is clearly up to no good

Photo: DND

The primary roll of the Argus was ASW and to successfully conduct an ASW mission, planning was critical. Knowing the target was key as it determined what tactics would be used. In the early days there were few nuclear submarines, so diesel search tactics were employed, usually using acoustic, visual and ESM sensors. These were passive tactics that usually did not alert the submarine to the presence of the Argus in the area. ETI was another tactic that was used. Search altitudes were a critical factor as effective ranges were different for the different sensors. If the tasking order directed that the aircraft remain passive and just track the submarine, then no active sensors, like radar or Julie would be used. As the number of nuclear submarines increased, they were less likely to make their presence known and passive acoustics, Jezebel, was the primary sensor.

Surface surveillance was another of the Argus missions that usually required the crew to identify and photograph all of the surface contacts in their patrol area. Normally the aircraft would enter the area at high altitude with radar on to locate all of the surface ships. The crew would then descend to identify and photograph each of the ships, logging their position, course and speed. If a ship was of particular interest the crew would do a full photo rig, getting pictures of both sides, as well as the bow and stern of the ship. Some surface surveillance missions were conducted passively to sneak up on a ship, usually a high interest vessel like a foreign intelligence gathering ship disguised as a fishing trawler.

An Argus crew member prepares a sonobuoy for deployment

Photo: DND

Above: LT J.D Preston, Navigator working on charts at the Routine Navigation Station on the Argus

Photo: DND

Routine Navigation

To patrol up to eight hours, 1,000 miles from land, the Argus required an accurate navigation system not only to transit to the tasked patrol area, but also to accurately report subsurface or surface contacts to maritime headquarters and other cooperating aircraft and ships. The heart of the Argus was the Canadian designed and built Air Navigation and Tactical Control (ANTAC) system. The ANTAC system was the most technically sophisticated navigation system of its time and provided effective navigation anywhere in the world, especially in the polar regions of the Canadian arctic.[1] It was considered to be the premier navigation system among all of the NATO contemporaries. The dead reckoning element of the ANTAC system's analogue computer used inputs of true airspeed, true heading, Doppler ground speed and drift to continuously calculate and display wind speed and direction, as well as latitude and longitude in real-time. In addition to verifying the above inputs to the ANTAC, the routine navigator periodically used celestial observations and Loran A[2] to update the displayed geographic position.

Below: Argus 719 from 415 Squadron flies over Newfoundland enroute to her home base at CFB Summerside, PEI after another long patrol

Photo: DND

---

[1] Navigation in the polar region is difficult because proximity of the Magnetic North Pole causes gross inaccuracies in magnetic compasses. Mechanized navigation systems also had difficulty tracking the high rate of changes in longitude at high polar latitudes.

[2] LORAN A was a shore-based long range radio navigation fixing aid

Tactical Navigation

The tactical element of the ANTAC computer displayed the aircraft's current position and velocity in the form of a light symbol projected onto the tactical navigator's chart of the search area. The position of the moving symbol allowed the tactical navigator to correlate the position of the aircraft with other tactical information plotted on the chart and to provide tactical direction to the crew. The tactical navigator had the ability to freeze the light symbol and slew it to any location on his chart to determine bearings and ranges. The resultant bearings and ranges automatically provided the pilot steering commands and distance to the point of interest selected by the tactical navigator. When the light symbol was unfrozen it would jump to the current position computed by the ANTAC.

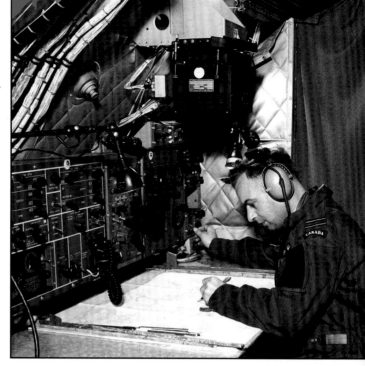

405 Squadron Tactical Navigator, F/L George Poll, plotting information provided by the sensor operators.

Photo: DND

Sound System Underwater Surveillance

Similar to the North American Air Defence Command's (NORAD) and Distant Early Warning (DEW) line of arctic radar sites provided warning against air attack, the U.S. Navy's (USN's) shore-based Sound System Underwater Surveillance (SOSUS) proved to be remarkably effective in providing long-range warning of Soviet submarine and surface targets approaching the coasts of North America. The Americans were keen on Canadian participation in the SOSUS system because the great circle route from Soviet naval bases in the Barents Sea to the American eastern seaboard passed through the Canadian area of responsibility. SOSUS operated on the same principles as Jezebel, but instead of using sonobuoys the SOSUS system used arrays of hydrophones planted on the ocean floor to detect submarine sounds. But more so than Jezebel, SOSUS was cloaked in secrecy and knowledge of its existence was limited strictly to those on a need to know basis. Similar to the

Crew members from VP 404 Squadron manning the various sensor stations inside the Argus

Photo: DND

725 drops a depth bomb from her aft bomb bay

Photo: DND

NORAD system, Canadian based SOSUS stations were jointly manned by Americans and Canadians, with Canadian personnel being drawn from Argus aircrew and Navy personnel with Jezebel qualifications. In the same vein that NORAD required interceptors to respond to DEW line penetrations, maritime commanders required ships and aircraft to react to SOSUS detections of Soviet naval combatants entering the western Atlantic. In the event of increased Cold War tensions, Soviet submarines in the western Atlantic posed a double threat. First, they were well positioned to interdict the sea lines of communication critical to reinforcing NATO forces in Europe and secondly, they were near their war stations from where they could launch Submarine Launched Ballistic Missiles (SLBM's) against strategic targets in North America.

737 is seen here patrolling over the eastern entrance to the Northern passage. Soviet nuclear submarines could stay under the ice for weeks on end

Photo: DND

After making the initial submarine detection, the aim of SOSUS was to direct a ship or aircraft to the Submarine Probability Area (SPA). Since submarines are extremely elusive, the probability of SOSUS putting a ship or aircraft in contact with a submarine decreased with the lateness of the reaction vehicle arriving at the SPA. Consequently, aircraft with their speed and range advantage were by far the preferred immediate reaction vehicle. Similar to the CF-100 interceptors assigned to NORAD, Argus aircraft maintained a two-hour alert, 24 hours per day, 365 days per year to react to a SOSUS hostile detection in the Canadian area of responsibility. The success of the SOSUS system depended on secrecy and stealth to ensure the enemy remained unaware of its capabilities. In addition to its speed, an aircraft had the advantage of being able to operate covertly over a SPA, whereas the noise from a ship's screws alerted the submarine to its presence.

An Argus on "2 Hour Alert" torches her number 1 engine during a pre-dawn engine start before she takes off on another mission in search of the Soviet threat

Photo: Wayne Griffith

The Argus/SOSUS team was Canada's most capable strategic ASW asset. The Argus' attributes complemented SOSUS better than any other reaction vehicle; its range provided the capability to react to SOSUS's long detection ranges, its speed minimized time late at a SPA and its endurance enabled the Argus to remain over a SPA longer than any other aircraft of its era. Increased time on top of the SPA increased the probability of gaining contact, identifying and tracking the intruder.

The Argus/SOSUS team members were mutually dependant on one another as individually neither

When not monitoring the flight instruments, the pilot and copilot of the Argus scanned the horizon for any sign of surface contacts

Photo: Lief Wadelius

When fully loaded the Argus could carry ,lbs of torpedoes, depth charges or sea mines

Photo: Greenwood Aviation Museum Collection

was as effective as when they worked together. To maintain the team's synergy, the complex hand in glove operation had to be continually practised. During training missions, a cooperating SOSUS station would search for a suitable training target. Obviously, a submarine would be an ideal target but these were rarely available for training purposes. Consequently, the SOSUS station had to resort to finding a suitable merchant ship to simulate a submarine. Once SOSUS selected a suitable target, the location and size of the pseudo SPA were transmitted to the Argus along with the components of the target's acoustic signature so the crew could identify the target by its acoustic fingerprint.

On receiving the target information the Argus, relying on its ANTAC and Jezebel systems would search the SPA with a pattern of sonobuoys. The search continued until Jezebel detected an acoustic signature that resembled the acoustic information sent from the SOSUS station. Because of different temperature profiles in various parts of the ocean the target noise detected by SOSUS arrays and the Argus sonobuoys often arrived via different sound transmission paths. Consequently, the acoustic signature detected by the Argus was seldom identical to the SOSUS signature. However, if the target was geographically within the SPA and there was good correlation between the two signatures, SOSUS was considered to have successfully put the Argus in contact with the target.

To foster the synergy between aircraft and SOSUS, Argus crews regularly visited the various SOSUS stations to better understand the SOSUS operators' techniques and challenges in generating a SPA. Similarly, SOSUS personnel often accompanied Argus crews on their SOSUS training flights to gain a better appreciation of how the Argus crews converted a SOSUS SPA into a prosecutable detection.

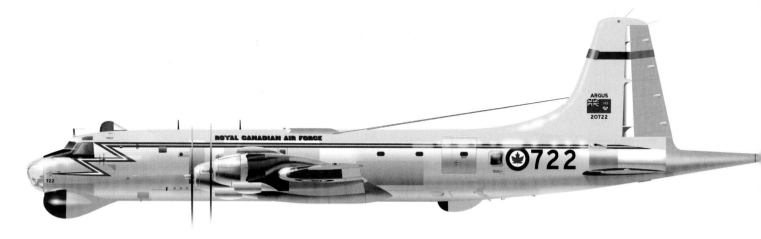

The last of the 13 Argus Mk I aircraft produced was 722. This marking scheme featured the more familiar and standardized quad reversing fuselage flash and Red Ensign on the vertical tail. This aircraft later served with 415 "Swordfish" Squadron in the 1960's and was later transferred to Comox, BC to 407 "Demon" Squadron.

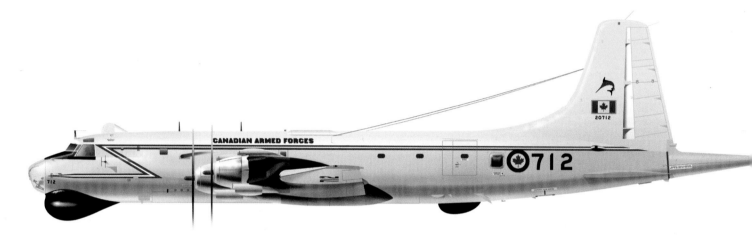

After RCAF unification into the CAF in 1968, aircraft fuselages were marked with bilingual text above the fuselage flash. The RCAF era roundel and last three digits of aircraft serial number were retained but the Starboard fuselage side wore English "Canadian Armed Forces" markings. The Port side of the aircraft featured the French equivalent of "Forces Armees Canadiennes". This scheme was short-lived due to a violation of ICAO rules and it was soon changed. Post 1973 aircraft featured the standard "CANADA" word mark and bilingual roundels. 712 and 719 were the last 2 mark I aircraft to fly with 415. By 1973 415 operated the Mark II exclusively.

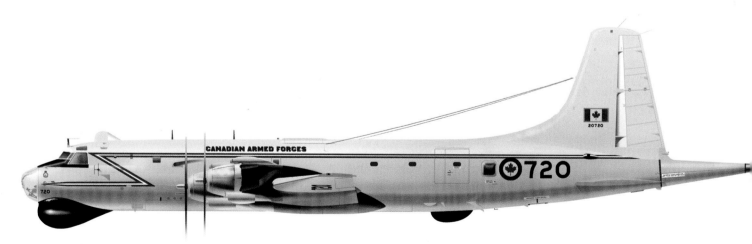

Argus 720 finished her career on the West Coast with 407 "Demon" Sqn. All newly transferred 407 aircraft soon featured Yellow prop spinners and a Winged Trident motif on the vertical tail.

The Hunt of the Mighty Argus

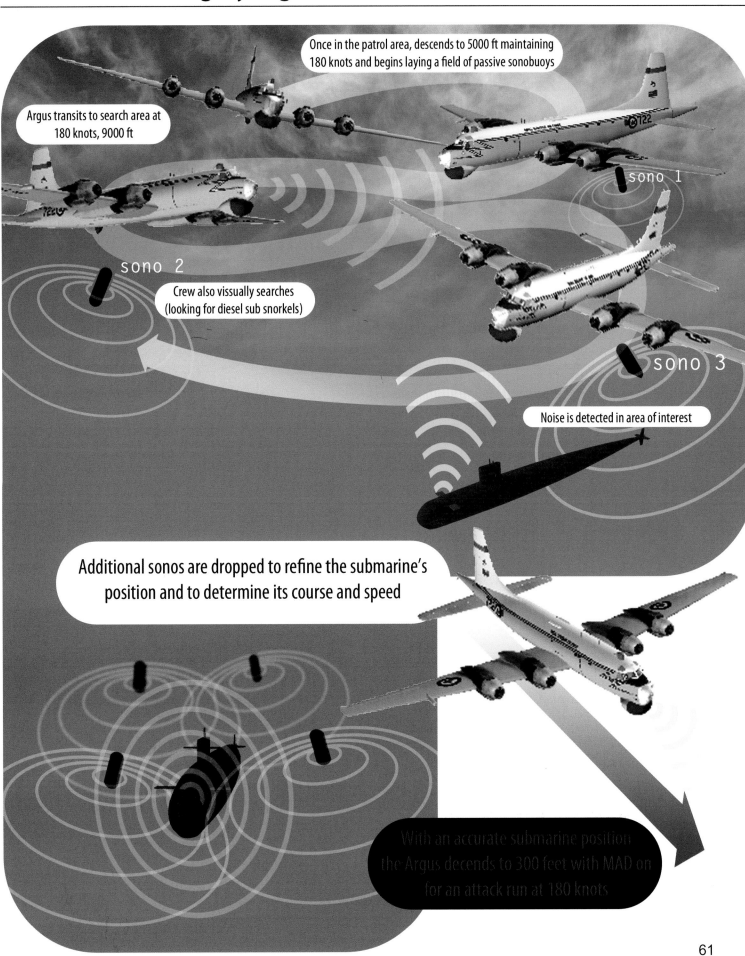

Once in the patrol area, descends to 5000 ft maintaining 180 knots and begins laying a field of passive sonobuoys

Argus transits to search area at 180 knots, 9000 ft

sono 1

sono 2

Crew also vissually searches (looking for diesel sub snorkels)

sono 3

Noise is detected in area of interest

Additional sonos are dropped to refine the submarine's position and to determine its course and speed

With an accurate submarine position the Argus decends to 300 feet with MAD on for an attack run at 180 knots

With a Mad Mark the Argus would drop two Mark 44 torpedoes or one Mark 46 torpedo then do a turn and begin an 1800 yard mad hunting circle looking to gain another Mad Mark as the submarine tried to escape.

MAD on

MAD on

1x Mk46

MAD on

2x Mk44

MAD on

During the attach runs, the Argus crew watches and listens to the acoustic information to hear an explosion or determine what evasive manoeuvres the submarine is taking to try and get away. Tracking continues until another attack can be made. Argus speed is constant 180 knots.

"Out of the Murk"

Painting: Rob Arsenault

From a Canadian sovereignty perspective, the Argus was the first RCAF aircraft with sufficient range to patrol any segment of Canada's coastline, including the arctic, from any base in Canada. Similarly, the Argus' exceptional endurance gave it the capability to survey vast ocean areas within the Canadian Economic Exclusion Zone (EEZ) in a single mission. These surveillance flights gathered unprecedented amounts of intelligence that were shared with other government departments, who used the information to ensure that no activity was contrary to Canada's economic well being or sovereignty. Knowledge of domestic and foreign fishing activity in Canadian coastal waters was of special interest to those agencies enforcing marine and fishing regulations. However, during the Cold War, knowledge of the disposition and latent threat posed by the Soviet fishing fleets would be militarily indispensable if East-West relations deteriorated.

The Defence of North America

The Argus' extremely long range and endurance was tailor-made to conduct surface surveillance off Canada's coasts. Not only does Canada have the longest coastline in the world, but the continental shelf off Canada's east coast is also the world's largest and richest in natural resources. Argus crews played an important role in patrolling Canada's maritime frontiers to ensure Canadian sovereignty was respected in our territorial waters and in our Exclusive Economic Zone (EEZ). The Argus logged thousands of hours in the mundane but important task of locating and reporting the activities of the very extensive foreign fishing fleets in our EEZ. In the Cold War era the Warsaw Pact countries had the largest presence in our EEZ and garnered the most scrutiny because in the event of hostilities their fishing vessels, which the Soviets centrally controlled, would be a tremendous intelligence-gathering asset and an innocuous re-supply resource for naval combatants. These fleets not only landed the largest fish catches but also harboured Electronic Intelligence (ELINT) vessels disguised as fishing trawlers. The ELINT trawlers

In addition to the Soviet submarine threat, Soviet fishing trawlers often gathered intelligence off the coast of Canada and it was the job of the Argus to counter that threat (as seen here in 1965)

Photo: DND

surreptitiously extracted intelligence from the full radio spectrum ranging from commercial radio broadcasts to marine and military communications. The Argus was the major contributor to the compilation of the Soviet presence. Continuous surveillance of the inauspicious fishing fleets off our coasts portended Soviet intentions and in the event the Cold War turned hot, knowing the extent of this latent enemy off our coasts would be critical to its early elimination.

Being one of only two types of aircraft that had the range and endurance to fully exploit the extreme detection ranges of the U.S. Navy's highly classified SOSUS system, the Argus played a major role in the

The Soviet surface and sub-surface threat in the mid-Atlantic was a shared responsibility between the USN and the RCAF. The Argus would often deploy to forward operating bases in Iceland and operate with P-3 Orion counterparts (1966)

Photo: DND

Argus Mk I with 405 "Eagle" Sqn, CFB Greenwood, NS circa 1978

Profile Drawing: Rob Arsenault

maritime defense of North America. The Argus/SOSUS team arguably prosecuted more Soviet penetrations of North American frontiers than their NORAD (North American Aerospace Defence Command) brethren. However, because the SOSUS system relied on secrecy and covertness for its success, Argus crews received none of the publicity or visibility of their NORAD contemporaries. Yet, they had played an equally important deterrence role in the Cold War by demonstrating a strategic presence over the North Atlantic. More importantly, the Argus and its crews' ability to maintain the secrecy of its partnership on the Air/SOSUS team for over twenty years proved Canada to be a trusted reliable ally in the maritime defense of North America.

The Cuban Missile Crisis

During the Cold War, the Argus contributed to the strategic maritime balance by routinely conducting random anti-submarine patrols in Canada's NATO area of responsibility. One of the by-products of these patrols was the reporting of all surface traffic encountered, including the regular flow of Soviet cargo ships en route to Cuba. In October 1962, when American intelligence gleaned that Soviet ships were transporting ballistic missiles to Cuba, only 90 miles from continental USA, the entire U.S. Navy Atlantic Fleet put to sea to form a blockade against the missile-laden ships. Similarly, the RCN put all of the resources that it could muster to sea, as did RCAF's Maritime Air Command. The world was on the precipice of a Third World War. Prime Minister Diefenbaker had to be coerced to abide by the NORAD treaty by placing the RCAF component of NORAD at DEFCON 2 (Enemy attack imminent); however, Diefenbaker could not be convinced to put maritime forces on an equivalent alert status. Consequently,

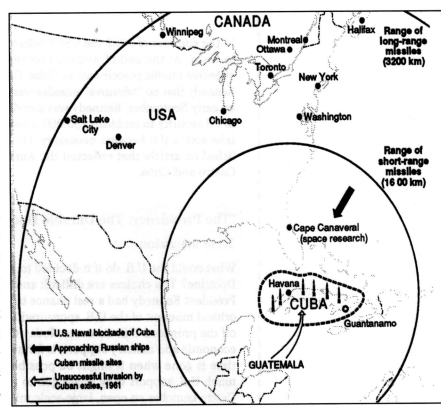

Golf II Soviet Submarine photographed by an Argus
Photo: Greenwood Aviation Museum Collection

authority to assist our American ally in searching for the Soviet ships was never issued and the rules of engagement including the release of weapons at sea, in accordance with DEFCON 2, were never promulgated. Without the support of the government, the Canadian Chief of Naval Staff, Admiral Rayner, could say nothing to Admiral Dyer, his Atlantic Fleet commander in Halifax,[1] other than, "Do what you have to do".

Ingeniously, Admiral Dyer immediately activated a "national" exercise scheduled for November. Although not authorized, Admiral Dyer invoked operations plans, which called for a "Sub-Air Barrier" across the Greenland-Iceland-UK gap.[2] With the agreement of the USN, Canadian planners moved the Sub-Air barrier farther

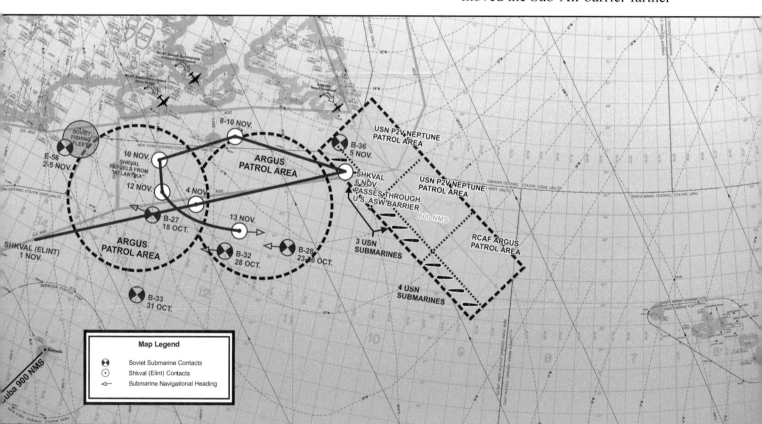

This map shows the extent of the Soviet threat during the Cuban Missile Crisis. Without the help and support of the RCAF and its Argus fleet, the USN would have realized serious coverage deficiencies (1962)

Illustration: Bruce Gormely

[1] The RCN and the RCAF's Maritime Air Command established a joint headquarters in Halifax to harmonize and coordinate their operations at sea. Most RCN operations automatically included Maritime Air Command.
[2] A Sub-Air barrier involved submarines and aircraft jointly establishing a barrier through which enemy forces must penetrate.

An RCAF Maritime Air Command CP-107 Argus links up with a USN P-2H Neptune at the outer edge of their respective patrol areas
Photo: Greenwood Aviation Museum Collection

south to extend from Cape Race, NL, some 600 miles southeast, to a point 300 miles from the Azores. For the first two weeks, 24 Argus from Greenwood were divided between surveillance and barrier patrols to locate and track Soviet ships and submarines. Eight more Argus later joined from Summerside. The Argus's, with their much longer range, were the key players from the start. They were the only aircraft able to cover the far southeast end of the barrier, a 1,000 miles from Greenwood. Three Argus were continuously on station, six hours out, eight on station and six hours back, twenty hours per flight. They carried full war loads, 8,000 pounds of Mk-54 depth charges and Mk-43 torpedoes. Torpedo batteries were even charged; an irreversible and expensive process and hundreds of sonobuoys were dropped. When sonobuoy stocks ran low, the USN flew in an extra 500 at no cost! But at no time did the RCN or the RCAF's Maritime Air Command go officially to a higher degree of military vigilance than DEFCON 5. Canadian ships and aircraft patrolled with the Master Armament Switch in the "ARMED"[3] position but had no authority to release any weapons. Because it lacked political authority Canadian participation was not displayed on the USN's status boards and maps in Washington. Commodore J.C. O'Brien, the Canadian naval attaché in Washington, did everything to ensure that the USN's most senior officers were aware of Canada's unofficial commitment. There were no official communications

20736 During early morning patrol drops two torpedoes

Painting: Rob Arsenault

[3] A critical enabling step in a series of actions to release weapons from an aircraft or ship

between Halifax and Ottawa. Admiral Dyer kept Admiral Rayner informed only by telephone.

Defence Minister Harkness kept the information to himself despite his knowledge of Diefenbaker's opposition to Canada's participation in the Cuban blockade. The RCN and the RCAF's Argus' stood alone honouring Canada's duty to stand by her North American ally, without one scrap of paper, memo, minute or message, or one public announcement to give it direction or approval.

The USN's "Historical Account of the Cuban Crisis" has no mention of Canadian operations. But those few who really knew what the Canadians had done also knew it lacked political authority. USN Vice Admiral "Whitey" Taylor, who commanded anti-submarine forces in the Atlantic, thanked his Canadian counterparts most sincerely, but only by classified messages and personal calls. The Argus' finest hour in which it played a key role in defusing a crisis that had brought the world to the brink of war passed unheralded.

Argus 729 before it was transfered to MP&EU

Profile Drawing: Rob Arsenault

PERSONAL ARGUS MEMORIES OF THE CUBAN MISSILE CRISIS

F/L Norman Donovan

In the fall of 1962 I was a Staff Instructor at JMWS, Stadacona, Halifax. One of my duties involved lecturing on the Canadian War Plans, NATO and CANUS Operation Orders, thus I had a good knowledge of the military plans and procedures that would be activated during each of the Readiness Conditions. These conditions would be set according to International events taking place. Normally the RCAF condition was DEFCON 5 during normal Cold War activities.

Yearly, NATO staff would conduct paper exercises during which we would test the various plans and operation orders. In other words we would fight WW3 on paper.

In September 1962, the paper exercise, code name FALLEX 62, was expanded to actually deploy and test alternate headquarters to simulate that the principal headquarters had been put out of action. During this scenario my billet was Intelligence Officer at the Alternate MHQ that was established in Torbay NL. At simulated DEFCON 2 we actually moved to Torbay by RCAF Comet aircraft. For ten

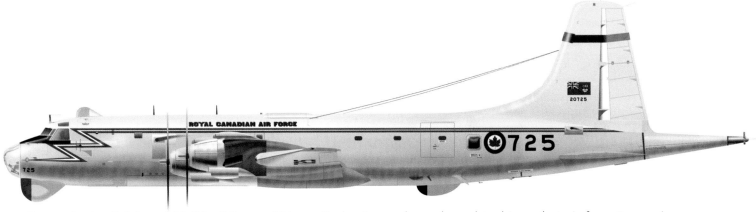

Remembering Sgt Angus.M. "Gus" Bower. This particular Argus always brought a big smile to is face. Prop spinners are still in 501-109 Grey and engine nacelles in Neutral Grey as well.

Profile Drawing: Rob Arsenault

days I manned the Intelligence Office on 12-hour shifts and we fought WW3. Quite an experience for a young navigator. Little did I realize that this was a rehearsal for what was to follow very shortly – The Cuban Missile Crisis.

On 22 October, I reported to JMWS for the evening shift in the Operational trainer. We were preparing crews from ships, air squadrons and submarines for a ten day exercise at sea. I arrived to find an empty parking lot, strange I thought. I was informed that the RCAF had set DEFCON 3 and all of our student crews had been recalled to their home units. I was to report to JMWS at 0800 next day for my orders. This was my introduction to the Cuban Missile Crisis. For the next 12 days I was on a four-hour standby to move to Torbay. Each day we were briefed at 0900 hours and 1700 hours on the daily events. My job was to digest the mass of message traffic and be prepared to open up the Alternate Intelligence Office in Torbay.

As the days went on, I became more and more aware of how serious things were getting. I was reading messages passing between the various headquarters, (USN, Halifax and Ottawa). The number of possible submarine contacts was mounting each day. How many Soviet submarines were there in the Western Atlantic? More and more aircraft were being sent on patrol. On 27 Oct, with the shooting down of the U2 aircraft I realized that the possibility of nuclear war could actually occur.

The ECM station was continually manned while on patrol

Photo: Greenwood Aviation Museum Collection

This is the only time that I ever discussed my job with my wife. When I deployed to Torbay she and my toddler son would be left alone in our house that was less than a mile from the Dockyard, which would have been a ground zero. I briefed her that when she dropped me at Shearwater to board the Comet, she was to proceed to her brother's house in Lower Sackville and stay there. His house had a deep below ground basement, well water and septics. We bought enough food and supplies for at least 30 days, although I realized that there would be no 30 days if nuclear war occurred.

Thank God both sides came to their senses and we reverted to normal Cold War Ops.

F/O Brian Wattie

At 16:45 hrs we were all immediately sequestered into barracks and the Crew Captains' wives went around PMQs and Hillcrest to collect clothing and overnight kit. I recall our crew of seven doing three long sorties; mostly surface surveillance and spotting at least one soviet freighter with the briefed type of containers on deck.

I do recall that after the first trip we were listening to the news that stated that the Prime Minister and Cabinet were convening to see what Canada's response would be. I wondered at the time if anyone had told them that we were already responding!

A USN Neptune on patrol links up with a RCAF Argus during the missile crisis

Photo: DND

F/O Bruce Montgomer

I really remember the Cuban Missile Crisis. I was a new navigator on Ken Waterhouse's crew, with Chet McNeil as TACCO and Leon Rushcall as Lead RO. We were on exercise Sharpsquall out of St Mawgan with Argus 741 in Oct 1962. Following the completion of the exercise we were ordered up to RAF Northolt to allow EMI Cossor to implement some modifications to the APS Radar. With a lot of time on our hands we were billeted in central London at a bed and breakfast. The night that the Cuban missile crises exploded, Leon and I were wandering around Piccadilly Square and couldn't believe the scene. It was like a riot, all these screaming people shouting that WWIII was about to begin and passing out leaflets requesting all to head to ten Downing Street to protest the imminent destruction of the world in nuclear holocaust. When we got back to our lodgings we were told not to go to bed as the crew were heading out to Northolt for an immediate recall to Greenwood. Luckily no one missed the flight. When we landed at Greenwood we were instructed to head home, pick up clean laundry and get back to the Reflex quarters. The dependents were being told to stock up on canned goods in case the balloon went up. All Argus were being armed with warshot torpedoes and depth charges. Basic Pilot/FE crews were assigned to those aircraft not assigned to maritime patrols to ferry these aircraft to less desirable airfield targets. Our crew flew our first patrol the day after returning from the UK. We flew four patrols during the episode. All the patrol operating areas were well to the southeast of Bermuda over the maritime approaches to Cuba. Most of the USN Squadrons on the east coast were equipped with the P2V Neptune which did not have the range. All our patrols were 17-20 hours.

Another interesting event at this time was that the Diefenbaker Government did not follow the US Government by implementing a higher state of DEFCON Alert. The two CF-100 Squadrons at CFB Uplands near Ottawa remained at normal standby and training status, parked wing tip to wing tip on the tarmac. I heard the following anecdotal tale during the aftermath of this crisis. It seems that a Committee of the US Senate was very critical of the Canadian Government for it's lack of action during this crisis. Apparently the USN Admiral who was SACLANT informed this committee that the Canadian Maritime Air and Naval forces responded in an effective and professional manner, since these units were under his NATO Operational control. SACLANT's intervention with the Senate Committee was said to have prevented a nasty note coming to the Canadian Government for it's lack of response to the Soviet's sending ICBM's to Cuba. However, as I stated, none of this can be proved, it was just anecdotal.

S/L Hi Carswell LGen (Ret'd)

When the United States revealed in the fall of 1962 that the Soviet Union was deploying Intermediate Range Ballistic Missiles in Cuba, it was clear that the inevitable confrontation could lead to war, possibly nuclear war. It was a very tense time, and the resulting confrontation directly involved Canada's Sea and Maritime Air Forces.

I was a fairly new Flight Commander with 415 MP Squadron in Summerside at the time, and very anxious to do a good job. There was a lot of speculation and rumour, along with a few facts. We didn't know which was which. President Kennedy was closely involved every step of the way, and the sensitivity and volatility of the situation prevented any useful flow of current information.

I had just come from a year at the Royal Air Force Staff College in the U.K., and it seemed like everybody there, except me, had been in one war or another, either in the Middle East, the Far East or Africa. I had felt like a greenhorn, so the prospect of possible combat action brought with it some excitement. In fact, all the Squadron members were enthusiastic about the idea of putting their extensive training to use in a "this is no drill" scenario. The crews were pumped to do well. No one seemed apprehensive, except for the fear of screwing up.

When not hunting Soviet submarines or surface vessels, Argus crews trained tirelessly with the RCN to hone their sub hunting skills
Photo: DND

The CP-107 Argus was Canada's first line of Maritime defence against the 1950's to the early 1980's. The 32 Argus aircraft, including 736 in the above picture amassed a combined total of some 500,000 hours patrolling Canada's coast lines and those of her allies.

Photo: Bert Campbell Collection

We had some knowledge of the antagonism between President Kennedy and Prime Minister Diefenbaker, although we didn't become aware of the intensity of their feelings until much later. Whether from that personal relationship, or from the traditional aversion of Canadian Prime Ministers to be seen to be taking orders from the U.S., the Canadian government failed to take any action to raise the readiness state of any of the Canadian military forces. There was an air of disbelief that with the two superpowers at each others throats, the Canadian government did nothing. Notwithstanding, the East coast Admiral, on his own, raised our state to Readiness State Bravo, one level short of all-out war. This intensified the excitement, and told us that our military bosses were very serious about the possibility of actual combat operations, and that they were darn sure they were not going to be caught napping.

On the practical side, Readiness State Bravo required a number of responses, one of which was to get all aircraft out of periodic maintenance and on the line. We had eight Argus on strength, and all were soon out of the barn and available for operations. In fact, to demonstrate our capability, the Squadron, with the inspiration of the Squadron Operations Officer, Slim Houser, sent all eight Argus over Greenwood in what might charitably be called a formation. Even in somewhat tense times, there was still a pressing need to get one up on our sister, and self-proclaimed, superior station, Greenwood.

The Americans had naturally moved their maritime emphasis to the south to set up for a possible total blockade of Cuba, so Canadian ships and aircraft moved to fill in the gaps. This meant more and longer patrols, all with fully armed aircraft. I remember going on a 24-hour patrol with Len Wilson and Crew 3. The patrol went fine and didn't seem too tiring, but when the hours of crew rest per flying hour was used up, nobody was very energized to take on another 24 hour trip.

Naturally there was discussion of the possibility of attacks on the U.S. or even Canada. Even those most prone to see the darkest side could not conceive of Summerside being on the target list. There was some concern though, that a nuclear exchange could lead to fallout in Eastern Canada. Many, somewhat surreptitiously, laid in extra food supplies, and at least thought about moving families out. I don't think anybody did. There was no official plan in this regard, and not even any suggestion, or even recognition that there was any potential danger for station personnel or dependants.

Good humour prevailed as always, and normal activities continued. But there was a palpable tension in the air as Squadron members recognized the seriousness of the situation, and the absolute need to rise to the occasion. Morale was high. Nobody complained of long hours, extensive flying or increased standby time. There was no problem getting volunteers for extra duty. When it was over there was relief that sane heads had prevailed and a sense of pride that we had done what was expected of us.

Many years later, when I was Commander of the Maritime Air Group, I accompanied Admiral Boyle to Norfolk. In a meeting of senior staff, the discussion turned to the risks of putting too much delegated authority in the hands of individual ship or aircraft captains or even task force commanders, in the nuclear age. Admiral Kidd, the Supreme Allied Commander Atlantic (SACLANT) told us that he had been the communications officer assigned during the Cuban crisis to relay the orders of President Kennedy direct to the U.S. forces in the Cuban area. The President was convinced that the situation was so delicate, and the stakes so high, that he could not risk the slightest miscalculation/ miscommunication or delay in the transmission of his direction. So there was to be one communications officer and no other intermediary between the President and the on-scene commander. It brought home to me in this discussion just how critical the situation had been in 1962.

Cuban Missile Crisis Summary

While no shots were fired from the US or USSR side, Canada's maritime role during the crisis should not be ignored or down played by historians. Had the situation escalated further, forcing the US to respond to the Soviet ICBM threat in Cuba, there can be no doubt that Maritime Command's East Coast Argus fleet was in an "unofficial" front line position to respond against any USSR submarine threat. While Canadians and the rest of the world sat watching the events unfold on the TV, few had any idea that the CP-107 Argus and her crews could have been asked to fire one of the first shots of World War Three. Thankfully they didn't but if they had, there can be no doubt that the USSR would have been facing a formidable aircraft for which there were few hiding places from, the "God with One Hundred Eyes".

If the "Balloon" had ever gone up, this was the last thing a Soviet submarine would have wanted to see when being hunted by "The Mighty Argus"
Photo: Greenwood Aviation Museum Collection

Photo: DND

Maintaining the Argus

When we look skyward and see a manmade machine in flight, some of us may just view it as a "million parts flying in close formation". Others may admire its majestic size, it's speed or perhaps it's aerial performance. The CP-107 Argus aircraft fit all these descriptions with the possible exception of speed. However, like any manmade machine, routine and preventative maintenance is required to ensure that all those "million parts" stayed in close formation in a safe and successful manner, allowing for a safe return to earth.

The Argus aircraft was huge in its day and could be very intimidating to both those that flew and maintained her. Having said that, maintenance on these "giants" was not a difficult task. The design was somewhat basic, no "fly by wire" or computer controlled systems as most large aircraft have today.

The normal maintenance of the Argus was carried out by highly skilled and dedicated aircraft trades men and

Technicians check an engine component to repair a problem found by the Flight Engineer

Photo: Bert Campbell

Argus 735 hooked up to an APU as ground crew talk to the air crew preparing to start the engines prior to another patrol while on deployment

Photo: DND

At the Argus Conversion Unit at RCAF Station Greenwood in Nova Scotia's Annapolis Valley, members of Maritime Patrol Squadron undergo training converting them from flying the Neptune to flying the new Argus. As well as the Pilots, Navigators, and Radio Officers, the Flight Engineers also undergo conversion training. Two of the Flight Engineer Instructors check over a chart for the de-icing equipment on one of the Argus's. Left, is Sgt. W. Neve, while on the right, pointing to an item on the chart, is F/S W. Tatarchuk.

Photo: DND

women, which consisted of an Airframe technician, an Aero Engine tech, Aircraft Electrician, a Safety Systems tech, a Weapons tech, a Communications and Radar tech and an Instrument tech. Because of the overlapping knowledge of the technicians, this created a team effort.

An accurate record of aircraft flying hours was maintained and at prescribed hours, the aircraft was "grounded" for either minor or major maintenance. Minor maintenance was carried out following each flight and in preparations for the following flight. Major maintenance involved a more detailed inspection of structure, components, systems and various components were replaced at this time as preventative maintenance.

One of the advantages the maintenance personnel had with the Argus was that it required a Flight Engineer when flying.

75

Argus Engine Bay crew on the 2nd of March, 1973. Jim Eyres, Jim Britten, Al Stoddard, Jess Vernier, Eye Ward, Richs Richards, Porkey Porquet, Vic MacDonald, Don Beck, Bob Cole and Fred MacDonald

Photo: DND

As the majority of the Flight Engineers were former Argus trained and experienced maintenance techs, this was an advantage when it came to post flight technical problems with the aircraft as they were able to fully describe the problems and provide all the necessary technical details that assisted the technicians in carrying out corrective repairs.

As stated earlier, the Argus was a large aircraft. The design however, was very good for an aircraft of its size. The manual flight controls seldom presented any rigging problems; the huge 18 cylinder engines (with 36 spark plugs) were reliable as were the electronics and mission systems. One often needed a ladder or maintenance stand to work on the engines and parts of the airframe but the advantages outweighed the disadvantages. Unlike some smaller aircraft, a technician did not have to be a "contortionist" to gain access to all the components and compartments required for maintenance.

Cpl Theobald, a Radar systems Technician i repairing a Doppler Radar Antenna in Gilbralta

Photo: DN

Though various Squadrons were allotted aircraft, maintenance was done by "central" maintenance, meaning that the maintenance personnel were not actually part of the Squadron. All aircraft received the same professional care regardless of the colour of the propeller spinners. (Each Squadron insisted on their colours, either being red, blue, green or yellow.)

Though all 33 Argus aircraft were built by the same manufacturer on the same production line, each aircraft was somewhat "different" from a maintenance point. The technicians got to know each aircraft and the unique technical problems that they may have had. Most of the fleet were very reliable and trouble free maintenance wise. However, there were some aircraft in the fleet that sometimes caused the "maintainers" to pull their hair out, resulting in some choice names for a couple of them such as "Miss Piggy", affectionately named after the high maintenance Muppet character.

Air Crew and maintenance crews prep an Argus prior to another mission

Argus technicians often found themselves working in some of Canada's harshest northern conditions without the luxury of a wind break or shelter

In the early and mid life era of the Argus in-service operations, obtaining spare parts did not create any serious issues for the "maintainers". Ample spare parts were held at the unit level as well as the various Supply Depots and third line Maintenance Contractors (IMP in Halifax). Even when deployed to a Foreign Service base, the maintenance technicians were able to "find" some necessary parts through the NATO parts cataloguing system.

However, as the Argus became older, one can appreciate that it would require more maintenance. (The maintainers would call it "tender love and care".) This in turn resulted in the necessity of more spare parts and components. But sometimes, because of its age, the parts began to dry up, and they became harder to find. There were many times when some parts had to be robbed from one aircraft for the health of another. The Argus and the CC-106 Yukon transport aircraft shared a lot of common parts, so when the Yukon was phased out of service, the common parts were saved for

LAC's Robert L. Brayley and Gerald G Maxwell prepare to start the four powerful engines of the RCAF's Argus sub-hunter against the backdrop of The Rock of Gibraltar. Ground Technicians with the RCAF's 405 Maritime Air Command Squadron of Greenwood, NS flew with the aircraft crew when NATO commitments took the aircraft to localities where local ground crews were not familiar with the aircraft.
Photo: DND

the Argus. But finding parts for the Wright-Cyclone 3350 engines was at times, a serious problem. Engine and airframe parts were not the only problem, some of the parts for many of the onboard detection equipment, radar systems and communications equipment was also getting out of date and hard to obtain.

Argus communications tech, AC Jim H. Bauder, Greenwood, repairing an inter-communication unit

Photo: DND

The Argus was designed to run on 115/145 grade aviation fuel. In the late 1970's, this fuel became harder and harder to obtain. As a result, through engineering, the ignition distributors were modified so we could use an alternate fuel of 100/130 grade. Of course, this reduced the performance of the aircraft as well as some minor long standing maintenance procedures, especially for the skilled and experienced Aero Engine technicians. To sum it up, it was through the resourcefulness and dedication of all maintenance personnel as well as the various supply sections that the Argus kept flying safely until its last flight.

When the Argus was deployed away from home, a maintenance crew consisting of a technician from each aircraft trade or sometimes only an airframe, aero engine and electrician was included. As stated, because of the

Pte Gary Saunders, an AE technician is filling the oil tank of the Argus aircraft

Photo: DND

of the skill level of all the technicians and cross knowledge of each trade, this procedure worked very well, and the Argus and her crews almost always got back home safely.

There were inherent problems with some of the various systems and components. Aero engine techs never had to change the oil in the air-cooled engines as oil typically "vented" all over the nacelles, undercarriage and fuselage and onto the ground. Apologies go out to the old Flight Sergeant that must have almost had a "compressor stall" when an Argus parked on the tarmac in front of the VIP Hangar at Uplands one time, and to the various control tower personnel that may have gone into a panic mode when they first witnessed an Argus starting up and smoking "just a bit" or sometimes witnessing the flames from the exhaust!

Operating the Argus in either a very cold or hot environment did not cause any particular maintenance problem with the various aircraft systems. There was never any requirement for maintenance on the oleo legs with the vast temperature spreads. The flight control systems as well as the hydraulic systems were basically trouble free in all temperature variances. If a hydraulic component looked like it was "bleeding", crews applied the "rule" that if it didn't leak more than 10 drops a minute, it was only "seeping". If there was a cut in one of the 10 tires and there was lots of tire tread remaining, tar from the expansion joints on the tarmac provided a good seal to prevent water and dirt from getting into the tire cord. These may sound like maintenance "secrets" but let it be known that all the technicians knew the limits of each aircraft and applied their skills and experience that maintained the fleet for over 25 years.

The Argus was well designed for their day, easy to maintain and respected by all that maintained and flew her. There are possibly many adjectives that could be used to describe this great aircraft, but tough like an old John Deere tractor seems to be the one that comes to mind for most of her maintainers. (Edited from original article provided by George White, 2009.)

Argus 726 on the tarmac at Kindley Air Field, Bermuda getting ready for start up

Photo: DND

An excellent view of two well oiled CP-107 Argus engines, number three and number four. Each engine produced 3,700 lbs of horse power.

Photo: Tom Hildreth

CP-107 Argus main right landing gear

CP-107 Argus right inboard flap in full down position

Photo: Tom Hildreth

Industrial Marine Products (IMP) Aerospace

For many years IMP, located at the Halifax airport, provided Depot Level Repair and Overhaul as well as Depot Level Inspection and Repair for the Argus.

In 1975, Argus 730 was sent to IMP in Halifax for destructive testing where the plane was taken completely apart to determine the state of its structure. IMP looked for structural fatigue cracks, corrosion and other faults in the airframe. Not too much was left of 730 when this photo was taken.

Photo: Barrie MacLeod

Inside the IMP hangar as an Argus goes through an overhaul
Photo: Barrie MacLeod

LAC M. E. Holland, a photographer at Greenwood, checks the F-24 camera installed in Argus before a flight

Photo: DND

RCAF Argus air crew are walked through the mechanical aspects of the mighty Wright R-3350 turbo compound piston engine

Photo: DND

Photo: Greenwood Aviation Museum Collection

Technicians get instruction using the Argus Flight Control System Trainer

Photo: DND

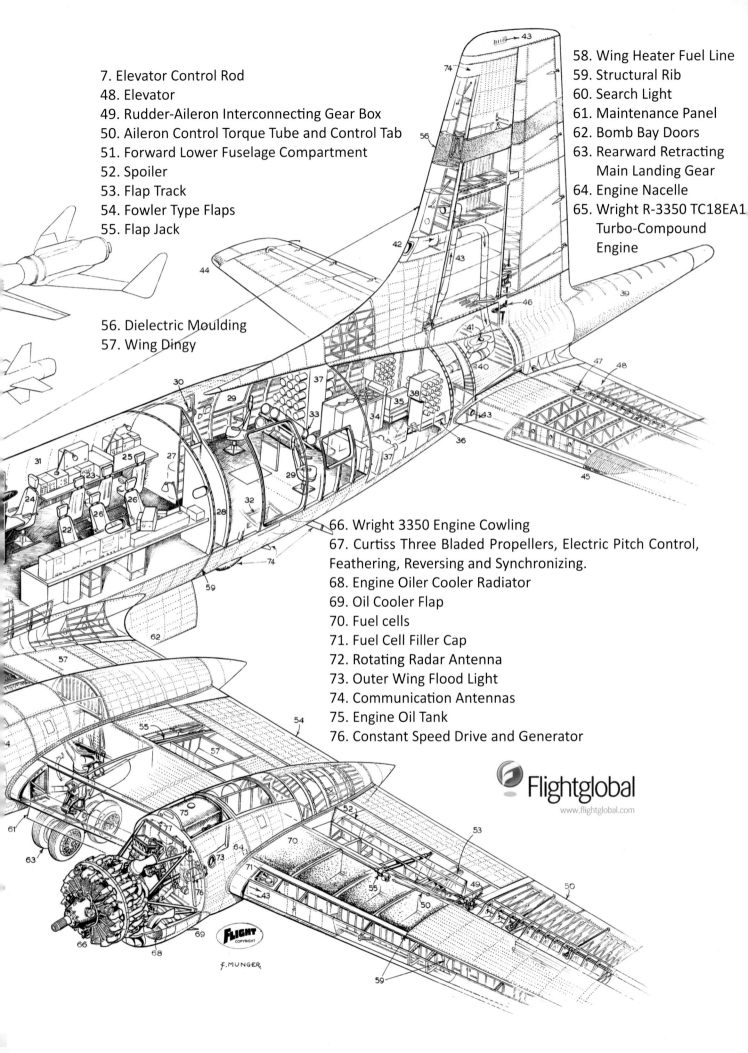

7. Elevator Control Rod
48. Elevator
49. Rudder-Aileron Interconnecting Gear Box
50. Aileron Control Torque Tube and Control Tab
51. Forward Lower Fuselage Compartment
52. Spoiler
53. Flap Track
54. Fowler Type Flaps
55. Flap Jack

56. Dielectric Moulding
57. Wing Dingy

58. Wing Heater Fuel Line
59. Structural Rib
60. Search Light
61. Maintenance Panel
62. Bomb Bay Doors
63. Rearward Retracting
    Main Landing Gear
64. Engine Nacelle
65. Wright R-3350 TC18EA1
    Turbo-Compound
    Engine

66. Wright 3350 Engine Cowling
67. Curtiss Three Bladed Propellers, Electric Pitch Control,
Feathering, Reversing and Synchronizing.
68. Engine Oiler Cooler Radiator
69. Oil Cooler Flap
70. Fuel cells
71. Fuel Cell Filler Cap
72. Rotating Radar Antenna
73. Outer Wing Flood Light
74. Communication Antennas
75. Engine Oil Tank
76. Constant Speed Drive and Generator

Flightglobal
www.flightglobal.com

F. MUNGER

FLIGHT
COPYRIGHT

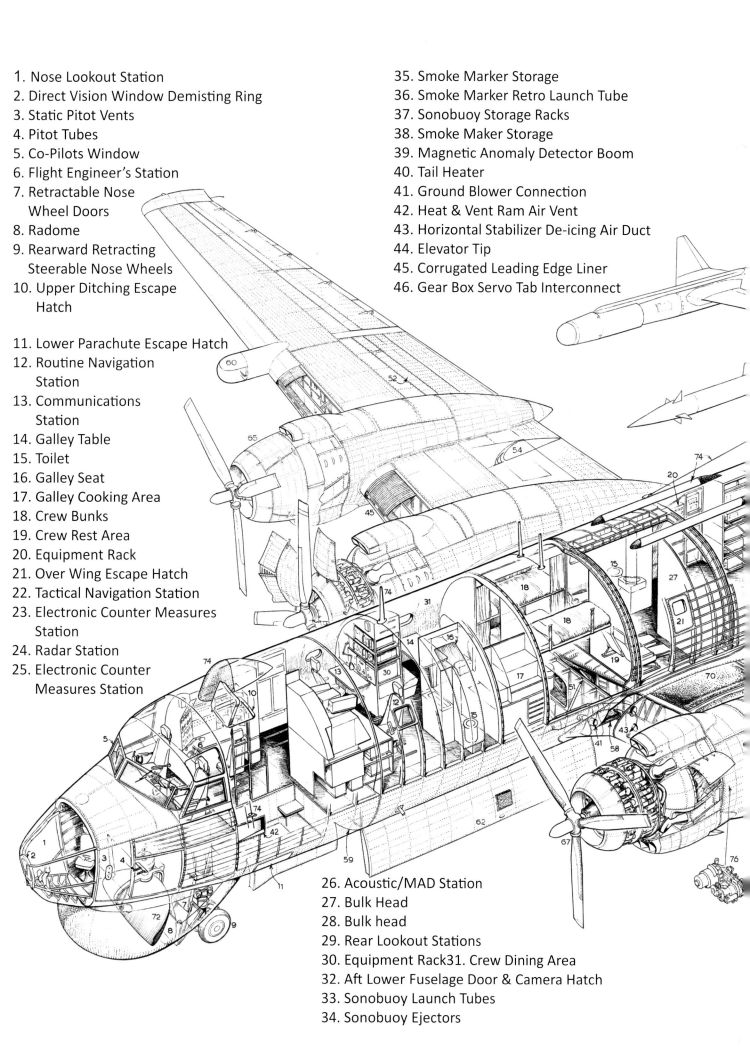

1. Nose Lookout Station
2. Direct Vision Window Demisting Ring
3. Static Pitot Vents
4. Pitot Tubes
5. Co-Pilots Window
6. Flight Engineer's Station
7. Retractable Nose Wheel Doors
8. Radome
9. Rearward Retracting Steerable Nose Wheels
10. Upper Ditching Escape Hatch

11. Lower Parachute Escape Hatch
12. Routine Navigation Station
13. Communications Station
14. Galley Table
15. Toilet
16. Galley Seat
17. Galley Cooking Area
18. Crew Bunks
19. Crew Rest Area
20. Equipment Rack
21. Over Wing Escape Hatch
22. Tactical Navigation Station
23. Electronic Counter Measures Station
24. Radar Station
25. Electronic Counter Measures Station

26. Acoustic/MAD Station
27. Bulk Head
28. Bulk head
29. Rear Lookout Stations
30. Equipment Rack31. Crew Dining Area
32. Aft Lower Fuselage Door & Camera Hatch
33. Sonobuoy Launch Tubes
34. Sonobuoy Ejectors

35. Smoke Marker Storage
36. Smoke Marker Retro Launch Tube
37. Sonobuoy Storage Racks
38. Smoke Maker Storage
39. Magnetic Anomaly Detector Boom
40. Tail Heater
41. Ground Blower Connection
42. Heat & Vent Ram Air Vent
43. Horizontal Stabilizer De-icing Air Duct
44. Elevator Tip
45. Corrugated Leading Edge Liner
46. Gear Box Servo Tab Interconnect

In order to accommodate its exceptional endurance the Argus always carried sufficient crew members to actually form 1 ½ crews. Each Argus crew consisted of three pilots, two flight engineers, three navigators and seven radio officers. The manning concept allowed each of the four crew trades to work on a staggered duty schedule that ensured there was always someone on watch who was current with the tactical situation. The navigators, for example, were on duty for four hours followed by two hours rest while the pilots worked three hours followed by 1 ½ hours rest. Off duty crewmembers ate in a well-equipped galley and rested in an area equipped with four bunks.

718 Training flight off the coast of Nova Scotia

Photo: Ken Wright

Argus Aircrew Training

Training of *Argus* aircrew began in Greenwood in April of 1958 with the stand-up of a detachment of the 2 Maritime Operational Training Unit (2(M)OTU) located in Summerside, PEI. The detachment, then called the *Argus* Conversion Unit (ACU) was established to convert P2V7 *Neptune* aircrew to the new CP107 *Argus,* with all the ground school taking place in 6 Hangar. The first Commanding Officer was Wing Commander Cy Torontow. The first aircraft assigned to the detachment was 716 followed by 718 and 719.

Argus 726 on a training flight

Photo: DND

The 6 Hangar housed a number of trainers including the Crew Tactical Procedures Trainer (TCPT) and the Operational Flight Trainer (OFT), both built by CAE. The TCPT was used for crew tactical training. The TCPT was outfitted with equipment and sensors that were identical to those on the aircraft and which were controlled by a number of computers to simulate actual mission profiles. The trainer itself was an exact duplicate of the *Argus* tactical, routine navigation and communications compartments. Students would prepare for each mission as they would for the real world, conduct the mission and hold a debriefing afterward. Instructors manned the computer consoles outside, the trainer controlling the mission and monitoring individual and crew performances.

Tactical Crew Procedures Trainer

Photo: Greenwood Aviation Museum Collection

The OFT was a replica of the Argus cockpit again computer controlled by instructors, for pilots and flight engineers. Unlike current flight simulators that have motion systems, the OFT had no motion capability. During the 70s there was an attempt to install the motion system from the Yukon simulator but it never worked properly.

The training of the *Argus* technicians was done by the 9 Field Technical Training Unit, also located in 6 Hangar. Their objective was to provide instruction to aircraft technicians on the location, operation and precautions associated with the various systems and services to the extent necessary for the proper servicing and maintenance of the *Argus* aircraft. They also provided assistance in trade advancement. Both aircrew and technicians shared a number of the part task trainers.

On April 1, 1968, the 2 (M) OUT in Summerside, the detachment in Greenwood and PFTTU(Page Field Technical Training Unit) were combined into the new 449 Maritime Training Squadron located in Greenwood. With the phasing out of the Neptune aircraft there was no longer a requirement to have a separate OTU I Summerside. They were disbanded on 29 August 1975, their duties being taken over by 404 Maritime Patrol and Training Squadron.

Argus Mk 1 20719 was also assigned to the ACU. Note the second unique fuselage flash and lettering. This aircraft also later served with 415 "Swordfish" Squadron until being transferred to CFB Greenwood. 404 "Buffalo" Squadron ultimately assumed responsibility for Argus crew training.

Profile Drawing: Rob Arsenault

Instructors man the console at the CP-107 Argus Tactical Crew Procedures Trainer in Greenwood, NS

Photo: Greenwood Aviation Museum Collection

Argus Squadrons

404 Squadron

404 Squadron at Thule Air Force Base, in Greenland

Photo: Leif Wadelius

404 Squadron received its first Argus on April 15, 1959. For the remainder of the year the Squadron's flight and ground crews trained to convert from the Neptune to the Argus.

Tragedy struck 404 Squadron in 1965 when Argus 727 plunged into the ocean during a night training exercise just off the coast of Puerto Rico. All crew members from the 404 squadron and one government research scientist died in the accident. It was a terrible blow to the Squadron and to Maritime Command.

Over the years the squadron flew a number of interesting missions. In 1972, while the Squadron was deployed on Trainex in Bermuda the whole Argus fleet was grounded due to a discovered landing gear problem. The four Argus on deployment were ordered to return to Greenwood and had to fly with their landing gear extended.

This 404 "Buffalo" Squadron Argus, from RCAF Station Greenwood, was observed in Winnipeg, MB in 1966 by Peter Mawle, a retired Air Traffic Controller from Summerside. Note the light Blue propeller spinners, lack of black outline on the early quad reversing fuselage flash and the post-1965 small silver maple leaf on the fuselage roundel. This aircraft and 20732 are the only Argus the Artist has ever seen in sporting this particular roundel.

Profile Drawing: Rob Arsenault

On August 29, 1975, 404 Squadron's roll as a Maritime Patrol Squadron was changed to the Maritime Operational Training Squadron. Most of the members of the Squadron were dispersed throughout the Air Force and the personnel & equipment of 449 Squadron were made part of 404 Squadron.

Over the years, over 1,000 aircrew and 2500 technicians were trained to fly and maintain the Argus and on 9 December 1979 the last Argus MOAT (Maritime Operational Aircrew Training) graduated. As the CO stated in his message to the graduates:

Argus 730 takes 404 crew to visit Winnipeg in July of 1969

Photo: Peter Mawle

Smokey start on Number One Engine prior to early morning takeoff

Photo: George Mayer

"The graduation of MOAT Course 7902 strikes a nostalgic note marking as it does the end of Argus aircrew and maintenance training. Since the introduction of the Argus over 20 years ago, thousands of aircrew and maintenance technicians have been trained in support of this complex yet sturdy aircraft. A proud record of achievement pays eloquent tribute to the success of its considerable training program . . . let us pay heed to the challenge of the Dawn of the Aurora – a challenge which invites us all to step into the future while keeping a clear eye on the past"

The last operational flight of an Argus by 404 Squadron took place on the 29th of August, 1980 when Major G.N. Holand and crew took Argus 10734 on a tour of the province of Nova Scotia.

Last MOAT Course

Photo: DND

404 Squadron Argus lined up while deployed to Gibraltar

Photo: Greenwood Aviation Museum Collection

405 Squadron

405 Squadron in the 1960's

Photo: DND

405 Squadron was the first unit to receive the *Argus*. Their first *Argus* flight was a test flight in 720 on August 7th, 1958. Their first flight with a full crew took place four days later. The first deployment was to Norfolk, Virginia from the 17th-20th of September in 1959 to show off the new aircraft. On June 2nd, 1959 the Squadron flew an *Argus* from Greenwood, NS to Shannon, Ireland and back, non-stop, setting an endurance record at the time.

In September 1969, Crew 7 of the 405 Squadron flew Ice Recce patrols for the giant American ice breaking oil tanker, the Manhattan as it made its way through the Northwest Passage, causing quite a political stir in Ottawa. Then in April 1974, the Squadron was deployed to Montijo, Portugal for "Exercise Dawn Patrol" when a military coup in the country grounded the aircraft. Crews were confined to the Portuguese quarters. After a few days, tensions eased and the squadron was permitted to fly back to Greenwood.

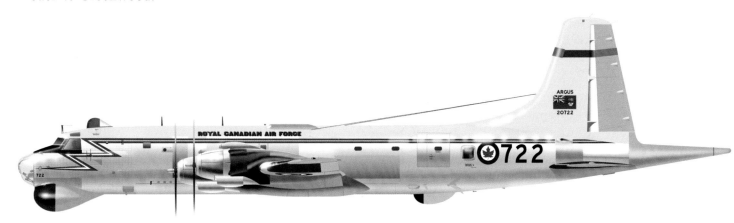

The last of the 13 Argus Mk I aircraft produced was 722. This marking scheme featured the more familiar and standardized quad reversing fuselage flash and Red Ensign on the vertical tail. This aircraft later served with 415 "Swordfish" Squadron in the 1960's and was later transferred to Comox, BC to 407 "Demon" Squadron.

Profile Drawing: Rob Arsenault

405 Squadron in Gibraltar, April 16th, 1959

Photo: Greenwood Aviation Museum Collection

The first successful MA1 (Deployable Survival Equipment) drop was made on June 27th, 1979 to an Irish adventurer attempting to cross the Atlantic in a 13 foot row boat. The crew were able to vector a ship to his location where he was rescued.

The last "real" Argus patrol by 405 Squadron was in 734 on the 11th of November, 1980 logging 16.8 hours.

405 Squadron gets their first operational Argus in 1958

Photo:DND

407 Squadron

Argus 718 and crew from 407 Squadron visit Japan in 1970. It was the first visit of the Canadian Military to Japan following the end of World War II in 1945.

Photo: DND

407 Squadron was the last unit to receive the Argus when 20711 arrived in Comox on May 17, 1968. For the next 12 years they flew 53,499 hours on the Argus. ASW deployments included Hawaii, Australia, New Zealand, Alaska, California and Japan.

On May 31, 1974 a 407 Squadron Argus departed Comox and returned the next day to establish an endurance record with a 31.1 hour non-stop flight that would have been longer were it not for re-tasking to a Search and Rescue mission in the first half of the flight.

407 Sqn, Comox, flew the 1st Canadian War Plane to Japan post WW II. The crew departed Comox on 19 January 1970, flying to Adak, Alaska, Tokyo, Nagoya and Hachinohe Japan, Midway Island (USA), arriving back at Comox 10 days later on 29 January 1970 in Comox. It was a diplomatic mission that went extremely well and the Japanese (Navy) were marvellous hosts and very professional airmen. The Captain of aircraft (718) was FL Ken Waterhouse

The last operational Argus flight from Comox was a Northern Patrol that departed on 29 June 1981 and returned on the 3 July 1981. The Argus served 407 Squadron well, both on the national and international scene around the Pacific rim.

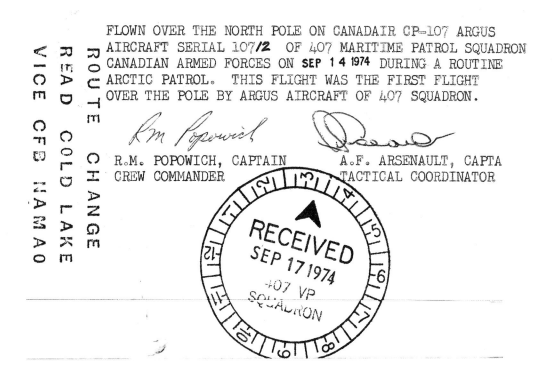

FLOWN OVER THE NORTH POLE ON CANADAIR CP-107 ARGUS
AIRCRAFT SERIAL 107/2 OF 407 MARITIME PATROL SQUADRON
CANADIAN ARMED FORCES ON SEP 1 4 1974 DURING A ROUTINE
ARCTIC PATROL. THIS FLIGHT WAS THE FIRST FLIGHT
OVER THE POLE BY ARGUS AIRCRAFT OF 407 SQUADRON.

R.M. POPOWICH, CAPTAIN   A.F. ARSENAULT, CAPTA
CREW COMMANDER   TACTICAL COORDINATOR

ROUTE CHANGE
READ COLD LAKE
VICE CFB NAMAO

RECEIVED
SEP 17 1974
407 VP
SQUADRON

Postcards used to document 407 Squadron's flight over the North Pole

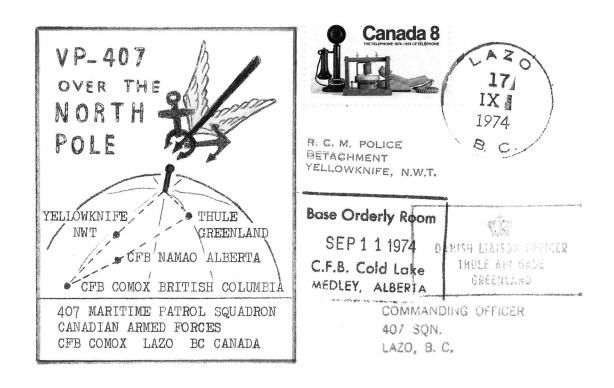

VP-407
OVER THE
NORTH
POLE

YELLOWKNIFE   THULE
NWT   GREENLAND

CFB NAMAO ALBERTA

CFB COMOX BRITISH COLUMBIA

407 MARITIME PATROL SQUADRON
CANADIAN ARMED FORCES
CFB COMOX LAZO BC CANADA

Canada 8
THE TELEPHONE 1874-1974 LE TÉLÉPHONE

LAZO
17
IX
1974
B.C.

R. C. M. POLICE
DETACHMENT
YELLOWKNIFE, N.W.T.

Base Orderly Room

SEP 1 1 1974
C.F.B. Cold Lake
MEDLEY, ALBERTA

DANISH LIAISON OFFICER
THULE AIR BASE
GREENLAND

COMMANDING OFFICER
407 SQN.
LAZO, B. C.

407 Squadron lined up in Comox, BC. Summer, 1978.

Photo: Mike Watson

The personal favourite of Albert "Satch" Szawara (aptly nicknamed for his 'trumpeter's chops'), 10711 served in Comox in the late 1970's. Like all 407 "Demon" aircraft, this bird sports Golden Yellow Propeller Spinners, a Winged Trident (from the Heraldic Crest) on the vertical tail and a Heraldic Crest on the Starboard side of the forward fuselage just below the cockpit. This airframe is also marked with the Blue and White Polar Bear marking depicting a Northern Patrol (NORPAT) bird.

Profile Drawing: Rob Arsenault

415 Squadron

VP 415 n the 1970's

415 Squadron received its first *Argus*, 720, on June 8, 1961 in Summertide, PEI. Shortly after, the Squadron set a Canadian endurance record flying non-stop for 30 hours and 20 minutes on Jul 26, 1961 during an Arctic Reconnaissance Mission. During the Cuban missile crisis the Squadron flew 25 *Argus* flights averaging 18 hours per flight without missing a beat. Following this event they put up two, four plane formations and did a flypast at Greenwood to demonstrate the high serviceability rate of the Squadron. During its first year they flew 3000 hours.

Over the years 415 Squadron flew on many memorable missions. One such trip was a Search & Rescue mission on the Newfoundland ferry, The William Carson that had hit an iceberg and was going under quickly. The 415 squadron provided night illumination with flares and their search light that assisted in the rescue of 126 passengers.

the 415 Squadron and MP&EU eight plane formation taxis by the Summerside tower on their way to Greenwood

Just prior to unification, the Argus marking scheme switched to a double reversing fuselage flash as depicted here on 20719 from RCAF Station Summerside with the Swordfish. The dielectric tail section, formerly flat Black and dark Grey, was switched to white at this time.

Profile Drawing: Rob Arsenault

Another mission was on Operation Morning Light, looking for debris from a Soviet nuclear powered satellite after it had re-entered the atmosphere and was scattered over large parts of the North West Territories.

1980 saw the squadron participate in the final Fincastle competition that an *Argus* would represent Canada. The following year, 415 Squadron began its move to Greenwood where they would end flying the Argus and start with the new *Aurora*.

On July 24, 1981, *Argus* 736, call sign "Sydney 02" took off from Greenwood, circled around then flew by the parade that was the 415 Squadron Change of Command, as a welcome to Greenwood and celebration of the last official flight of the Argus for 415 Squadron. Seven months later, a 415 Squadron crew flew *Argus* 742 to Rockcliffe, ON to the Canadian Aviation Museum where it is on permanent display.

Argus 736 of 415 Squadron visits Valkenberg, The Netherlands

Photo: DND

Argus 737 shows off her lines as she takes to the skies and continues to fly a nap of earth profile while her gear is retracted. Argus 737 was later lost in a fatal accident in Summerside that claimed the lives of three of her crew.

Photo: DND

The Argus frequently flew over Halifax and Maritime Command Headquarters when enroute or returning from a patrol. Here, Argus 723 from 415 Squadron flies over Halifax Citadel in the early 1960's.

Photo: DND

449 Squadron

On 1 April 1968, 449 Squadron was formed to incorporate five separate training establishments into one unit and included 2(M) OTU, the Argus Conversion Unit, Number 9 Field Technical Training Unit, the Operations Flight and Tactical Trainer and the Maritime Radar Trainer. The role of 449 squadron was too:

1. Train graduate aircrew to the basic standard of ASW operational efficiency required by a VP squadrons;

2. Train technicians in the maintenance of telecommunications, aero engines, airframes, electrical systems, instruments and weapons particular to the Argus;

3. Provide training facilities in radar, simulated flying and maritime procedures; and

4. Maintain an operational capability within the maritime command forces.

This squadron adopted the unicorn as its badge and like the creature itself, its abilities were derived from the strengths of the many parts from which it was composed.

Mr. Woodman, left, presented the "Unicorn" horn to 449 Squadron on the occasion of LCol John Bradley, middle, taking over command of the Squadron from the first CO, LCol Cal Rushton, right

Photo: Greenwood Aviation Museum Collection

Formed in 1968, some of CFB Greenwood's 449 "Unicorn" Training Squadron aircraft featured dark green propeller spinners. Argus Mk I 10717 featured this unique austentation when observed in September 1971. 449 "Unicorn" Squadron was disbanded in 1975 when 404 "Buffalo" Squadron assumed responsibility for Argus training.

Photo: Rob Arsenault

of ½

741 Climbs to the sky in 1966

Photo: Peter Mawle

While training was being conducted in Greenwood, a detachment of 449 Sqn was in Comox, BC converting Neptune trained aircrew to the Argus. In 1969, training of Naval Aviation Observers to replace the Radio Officers on the Argus began and their title was later changed to Airborne Electronic Sensor Operators (AESOP).

The last official flight of 449 squadron was on August 29, 1975, the same day the squadron changed its identity to 404 Squadron.

Crew of the last 449 flight
Photo: Greenwood Aviation Museum Collection

MP & EU visit to a US Naval Station in the late 1960's

Photo: Greenwood Aviation Museum Collection

MP & EU

During the early 1950's it became apparent that to protect Europe and North America from nuclear attack by the new generation of submarines it was necessary to greatly improve anti-submarine warfare (ASW) defences. This lead to research projects in Britain, USA and Canada to develop new ASW equipment and techniques. As new ASW equipment was developed it was necessary to evaluate it under operational conditions.

This testing was assigned to existing naval and maritime forces. In the RCAF's Maritime Command such testing was carried out by the newly formed Evaluation and Development (E & D) Flight of 404 Squadron at Greenwood. It soon became such a large commitment that it warranted the establishment of a specialized flying unit and as a result the Maritime Proving and Evaluation Unit (MP&EU) was born on June 1st, 1959. On August 1st, 1959 MP&EU departed its birthplace in Greenwood for RCAF Station in Summerside, Prince Edward Island where it would remain for 19 years.

MP&EU was established with one Argus aircraft and two Neptunes. The Neptunes were not used extensively for trials because of their cramped interior. The Argus on the other hand, was ideally suited for this purpose. She had ample space for installation of prototype equipment and ample electrical power available for testing. In addition, the Argus was capable of transporting the required personnel and equipment when deployed on detachment. Without the large Argus aircraft MP&EU's work would have been very difficult.

In 1978 MP&EU moved to CFB Greenwood, NS. After a long career, Argus 728 was flown from CFB Greenwood to storage in Summerside on the 3rd of October, 1979. The last official flight of the remaining MP&EU aircraft took place on June 25th, 1980 in Argus 729, and on July 4th of the same year, she was flown to CFB Summerside for final disposal. MP&EU is still situated at CFB Greenwood and continues to test new equipment for the Argus's replacement, the CP-140 Aurora.

The Longest Flight by Chris Charland

Argus 725 Taxis in after the longest flight

Photo: Chris Charland Collection

At 14:10 hours on the 2nd of October 1959, R.C.A.F. Station North Bay, ON was 'propelled' into Canadian aviation history. The Northern Ontario fighter station was the unscheduled terminus for a record-breaking 4,570-mile flight by a Canadair CP-107 *Argus* Mk-2 #20725, of 405 'Eagle' Maritime Patrol Squadron.

A pair of aircraft from R.C.A.F. Station Greenwood, Nova Scotia had been invited by the Australian state of Queensland's government to help celebrate its centennial. The Argus task force was commanded by Group Captain John Roberts. While there, the Canadians carried out a number of anti-submarine exercises with the Royal Australian Air Force, followed by some 'fun in the sun' at the famous Surfer's Paradise.

The Canadians left Brisbane and headed south to the country's capital Canberra, in the Australian Capital Territory. During their stay, they performed at a number of air shows as part of Royal Australian Air Force Week. From there, it was across the Tasman Sea to New Zealand. Their arrival coincided with the arrival of the Royal New Zealand Air Force Chief of Air Staff in Canada. While in New Zealand, the aircraft created quite a stir. People were fascinated by the sheer size of the aircraft that was named after the Greek mythological giant with a hundred eyes. Nine lucky members of parliament were treated to an aerial tour, winging their way from Christchurch to Wellington. More A.S.W. exercises were carried out, this time with their host country.

When it came time leave the Royal New Zealand Air Force Base Ohakea at Palmerston on the country's North Island, *Argus* 725 would be making the long trip back home alone, as the second aircraft developed an engine problem and had to remain in New Zealand until repairs could be made.

Argus 725 headed east for a stopover at Naval Air Station Barbers Point. The former United States

Navy facility is located at Ewa Beach on Oahu, 20 miles south of Honolulu. After a brief rest it was time for some record-setting flying. Next stop Ottawa. As a means of fuel conservation, the mighty four-engine sub hunter's heaters were shut down while en route. Things got rather chilly as they traversed the majestic snow capped Rocky Mountains at 13,000 feet in search of favourable winds.

Stronger than forecast headwinds caused higher gas consumption, which in time created a critical shortage of fuel. This prompted the crew to select North Bay as a way-point, which proved a wise decision. The station had less than an hour's warning time to prepare for the aircraft's arrival. Upon landing after being airborne for 20 hours and 10 minutes, they estimated that there was only one hour's worth of usable fuel left in the aircraft's tanks.

Meanwhile, back at Uplands, a big reception and party had been organized to celebrate the triumphant arrival of the *Argus* crew. News of the impending landing at North Bay and "NOT" Ottawa sent two T-33 *Silver Stars* from R.C.A.F. Stations Uplands and St. Hubert, scurrying to get to the 'Gateway City' taking Air Vice Marshal John Easton and Air Commodore W. I. Clements with them to welcome the return of the record breaking crew. The *T-Birds* arrived at North Bay moments before the touch down of 725.

The pair of high-ranking officers were in place as the *Argus* came to a stop in front of No.2 Hangar. Both were presented with traditional Hawaiian leis by Group Captain Roberts. They really must have thought a lot of these gifts as they wore them while marching with the crew past an honour guard. Easton and Clements were also presented with a model Fijian canoe. After a lengthy press conference, the crew were escorted by the station commanding officer and 'Saviour of Ceylon' Group Captain Len Birchall OBEDFC CD. Argus 725 and her crew departed North Bay the next day for Ottawa.

The crew of *Argus* 725 broke an existing speed/range record which up to that point had been held by another *Argus* crew from their squadron. The original record was set after an *Argus* flew non-stop from R.C.A.F. Station Greenwood to Ireland and return, for a distance of 4,210 miles. *Argus* 725 carried a total of 25 personnel onboard versus a standard crew compliment of 15 (although only 11 crewman flew this particular trip). It was not in any way modified for this occasions and carried its typical maximum fuel load "pretty impressive, what!". The Argus pilot then said, "Not bad. . . watch this". For the next 20 minutes the Argus flew straight and level. The fighter pilot was not impressed and asked, "So what did you do?" to which the Argus pilot said, "I got out of the seat, went back to use the washroom, grabbed a sandwich and coffee and chatted with the Navigator." There was no response from the Tomcat as it peeled away to head back to the carrier.

Air Vice Marshal John Easton is presented with a model Fijan canoe

Photo: DND

The crew of the longest flight pose in front of Argus 725

Photo: Chris Charland Collection

A Bad Day, That Was Trying to Get Worse . . . Quickly.
By Warrant Officer (Retired) Craig MacAusland, Tyne Valley, PEI

Crew 1, the "Gropers" of 415 Squadron were flying Argus 736 in the late 70's on what should have been a routine anti-submarine warfare (ASW) patrol. They took off out of RAF Kinloss, Scotland flew toward the Pentland Firth, and then on into the Greenland—Iceland—United Kingdom (GIUK) gap, a place notorious for The Soviet Red Banner Northern Fleet submarines heading out from the Barents and Norwegian Seas toward their patrol stations in the Arctic and Atlantic Oceans. The crew had held Prestwick, Scotland as an alternate airport with a possibility of Macrahanish, Scotland if required.

A few hours into the patrol, destination and alternate weather, actual and forecasted, continued to deteriorate. Due to fuel and time considerations, a decision to divert to Keflavik, Iceland was made, even though the wind was forecast to be high. I remember the start of the approaches, with Captain's Gary Baker in the left pilot seat and Mike Havel in the right co-pilot seat. The high winds slamming into the side of the Argus caused major buffeting as the aircraft approached minimum decision height. It was the first of many overshoots. The next three approaches became increasingly more difficult as the winds increased swinging the aircraft's nose to the right about 45 degrees at times. For anyone with a sense of flying in cross winds, the counter action required by the pilots to fly a safe approach is to angle the aircraft into the wind and use opposite rudder to keep the flight path straight. These necessary inputs had the aircraft approaching at 45 degrees off the centreline of the runway. At the precise moment of touchdown the pilot had to kick the rudder to swing the aircraft's nose onto the centre line of the runway. Landings were typically done by the guy in the left seat but as the weather deteriorated further, each approach now required both the pilot and co-pilot to be on the controls. Fuel had now become a serious consideration and after several more missed approaches, Flt Eng Ron Scott was heard saying over the inter-

Artist depiction of Argus 736 and Crew 1 "Gropers" attempting several landings in very heavy cross winds and rain after being diverted to Iceland

Painting: Rob Aresenault

com, *"Things are going to get very quiet up here"*. Gary's arms were dead after some serious "white knuckle driving". He had to get out of the left seat, and when he came to the galley for a break, he was literally soaked with sweat from the effort of trying to land the plane. Mike Havel was in the left seat now, and again had to overshoot. On the next approach, while most of the crew had the sensation that the Argus was flying sideways, the two pilots, at the very last second, with barely enough fuel for another approach, managed to carry out the landing at the cost of a couple of tires. All in all, a fair trade for a landing that every one walked away from.

Living High On Board The Argus by Geoff Bennett

If you look up the performance figures of the long-extinct Canadair CL-28 Argus Long Range Maritime Patrol Aircraft, one figure that stands out is its endurance. The Argus could remain aloft for as long as thirty hours, though normal patrols were routinely 12-18 hours long. Have you ever wondered how the crews kept body and soul reasonably operational on such flights? It required food, and lots of it.

Normal crew complement was 16, give or take some small variations, and they all needed a meal every four hours or so. That implies large scale catering, which was achieved by the dedicated, flexible effort by base food services and a fair amount of crew ingenuity. Rations were delivered in three wooden boxes the size of small coffins, cardboard cartons, and three or four large stainless steel water canisters. Rations included many loaves of bread, butter, various spreads, cold meats, fresh and canned fruit and vegetables, pre-roasted beef, raw steaks of good quality flats of eggs, cartons of milk and fruit juice, disposable utensils, an electric frying pan, etc. All this was delivered to the bottom of the aircraft ladder, at any hour of the day or night and often on very short notice. The aircrew lugged all this stuff up the ladder, and then forward to the gallery for storage.

A Routine Navigator enjoying a hot meal

Photo: Lief Wadelius

The gallery had stainless steel drawers, cabinets, cupboards, a refrigerator, and two-hot plate stoves equipped with a small oven. On the galley table stood a much-used two slice toaster.

Each crew had its own rations officer who kept a portable kit of goodies for emergencies and at least eleven secret herbs and spices. The rations officer ordered all the food, purchasing it at foreign bases, and took the blame when things in the catering line went wrong. Crews were large enough to allow a few members in each trade, pilot, flight engineer, navigator and radio officer (later observers), to be off duty in rotation. Those who were off duty slept or ate, so the gallery was the airborne social centre on an "out task" Argus.

Often the aircraft was filled with garlic-flavoured blue smoke, a byproduct of butter fried steaks, bacon, eggs and onions. This smoke played hell with the electronic gear (radar and other such stuff) that we used to fight the Cold War, but it was a handicap we gladly accepted. On my own crew we

Discussing the next menu

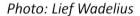
Photo: Lief Wadelius

had an S.O.P. (Standing Operating Procedure) whereby on those 'one-in-the-morning' launches, as soon as practicable, those off duty cooked a cholesterol-laden breakfast for all on board. There is nothing like a hearty feast of bacon and eggs, butter-soaked toast, and a hot coffee, all served up on a laptray in the cockpit as the sunrise cracks the horizon. From five thousand feet, eastbound over St. John's, NL, the early-morning world looks very good.

A gifted cook was an asset to a crew. I was fortunate to "own" a flight engineer who could whoop up a delectable clam chowder. Other crews boasted omelet-masters. We ate hearty on the Argus! On rare occasions of significance, when high-level brass were aboard, there sometimes appeared some illicit potent potables, but that is another story!

During most 18-hour patrols, the galley proved time and time again to be a great source of crew moral. Of course, this was always dependant on the designated crew chef.

Photo:George Mayer

117

Accidents "The Curse of the number 7"

Argus 727

On the night of 23rd March 1965, while deployed on exercise to Puerto Rico, 404 Maritime Patrol and Training Squadron Argus 20727 plunged into the ocean 60 miles north of the island. The entire crew and a government scientist perished in the crash. Given the lack of physical evidence, the true cause of the crash has never been determined.

The crew of Argus 727

Photo: Greenwood Aviation Museum Collection

In remembrance of those who paid the ultimate sacrifice in 404 Squadron Argus 20727—Ex Maplespring—23 Mar 1965

Photo: Rob Arsenault

Argus 717

On March 24, 1966, Argus 717 was on an authorized low-level mission over the Bay of Fundy to evaluate a camera recorder installed in the rear of the aircraft. Flight Sergeant R.W. Major, assigned as the second engineer, was found to be missing when a check of the aircraft and occupants was initiated shortly after the "Door Warning Light" illuminated on the cockpit instrument panel. The camera hatch was subsequently found to be open. The mystery of what happened to Sergeant R.W. Major was never solved.

Argus MkI with 405 "Eagle" Sqn, CFB Greenwood, NS circa 1979. This aircraft was spared from the wrecking ball and continues to serve as 17Wg Greenwood's largest Gate Guard.

Photo: Rob Arsenault

Argus 737.

On 31 March 1977, Argus 10737 crashed while landing in bad weather at CFB Summerside, PEI, : killing three crewmembers and injuring others.

Argus 737 had initially been assigned to a ship Search and Rescue mission, which was cancelled and then was reassigned to a routine operational patrol. Number 1 engine malfunctioned in flight and was shut down. Fuel was dumped to reduce the aircraft to landing weight and a surveillance radar approach was completed to runway 18 at CFB Summerside. At approximately a half mile from touchdown on course, the crew reported visually and were cleared to land. Witnesses in the control tower reported that the aircraft then nosed over rapidly, followed by an abrupt roundout. Power was applied and the aircraft began banking to the left while still descending.

Argus 737 seconds before her left wing sliced through the parked Nordair Electra

Photo: Gary H. Baker

Argus 737 narrowly misses the CFB Summerside Control Tower as her crew desperately try to control her. Note the feathered propeller on number one engine.

Photo: Gary H. Baker

From left to right: Major Ross Hawkes, MCpl Al Senez and Sgt. Ralph Arsenault were all killed in the crash of Argus 737

Photos: DND

The aircraft touched down on the left main landing gear in a nose high attitude in the infield 100 feet to the left of the bottom of the runway. After two touchdowns the aircraft became airborne again. The left wing continued to drop and the Argus flew in a curved path and crossed the ramp just in front of the control tower where it struck an unoccupied Nordair Electra parked on the apron. The left wing of the Argus severed the aft fuselage and ripped open the left wing of the Electra. The Argus crashed on the ramp, slid into the infield and bursts into flames. 15 of the crew manage to escape from the wreckage. An observer as fatally injured in the crash. Subsequently, the supervisory pilot and one flight engineer died from their injuries.

In remembrance of three crew members who paid the ultimate sacrifice in 415 Squadron Argus 10737 - 31 Mar 1977

Profile Drawing: Rob Arsenault

The Nordair Electra after the accident

Photo:Peter Mawle

Photo: Tom Gosling

Argus Mishaps

Failed brakes Argus 10740

On 18 February 1970, the crew of Argus 740 got up around 0430 for a 0700 take off from Puerto Rico to the sunny island of St. Croix for some R & R. All the crew, except the pilots and engineers, changed into their island finery enroute, so on landing they were dropped off at the Terminal as the aircraft was being parked further down the line. The line crew were told they needed bigger chocks than what they had on the line. While waiting for them, the remainder of the crew retired to the over wing hatch area to change out of their flight suits. They started to feel the aircraft sway a bit and mentioned it to the pilot. He said that it was just the wind. Suddenly the Flight Engineer saw a tree pass by the window and raced for the cockpit thinking the pilot forgot to set the parking brake. As he stomped on the pedals and pulled the brake handle he noticed a GPU passing under the nose which was followed by a crunching sound as the A/C ground to a halt on top of said GPU. On exiting the aircraft they found a damaged radar dome, bomb bay door, nose tire, and a GPU, which some how had got jammed sideways, sitting in the forward bomb bay. On examining the system, it was discovered that the main brake accumulator was unserviceable and had bled off all the brake system pressure. As they had been parked on top of a grade, when the brakes let go the aircraft started rolling and picked up pretty good speed over the next few hundred feet. Reporting back to base we were told that another aircraft would be sent over that night with ground crew to assess and repair out their aircraft. The relief aircraft didn't arrive until 2200 that night, ground crew said it would take some time before ours was airworthy so, as we had a 0200 take off for the exercise, we took the relief aircraft back.

Lost Propeller Argus 10739

In July 1971 as crew 4, 415 Sqn was starting up to leave Yellowknife after a completing a Summerside-Frobisher Bay-Yellowknife Northern Patrol. As the pilot depressed the start button, number 3 propeller came off the engine and chased the ground crewman about 100 yards down the tarmac. In the photos the crew took, you can see the propeller, under number four engine.

Argus 739 number 3 engine looses its prop
Photo:DND

Heavy landing Argus 10714

Note the gouged marks left on the runway after the hard landing in the picture on the right. Above you can see the warped propeller that occured as a result of hitting the ground during landing.

All photos: DND

As they say, a picture is worth a thousand words.

Gear Failure Argus 10740

Argus 740 with main landing gear problems

Photo: DND

Situation: Nose wheel and left main wheel down and indicating a safe, right main wheel hanging about halfway extended. No name hydraulic pressure. Various manoeuvres were tried in attempt to force the right main to lock down. Yaws were found to be the most effective manoeuvre. However, yaws alone were not enough the force the right bogey far enough forward to engage the down lock.

With 15° flat, 2600 RPM and an indicated airspeed of 130 knots, a series of wings level (or nearly level) yaws were initiated. When the maximum obtainable amount of yaw was reached quite a pronounced swing arc was produced on the right main bogey. The pilot was using full left and right rudder and an observing aircraft estimated that the degrees of yaw to be 30° either side of center. When the nose yawed to the left, the right wheel would swing back and up towards the nacelle and when the nose yawed to the right the wheel would swing down and forward toward the locked position.

On one series of yaws, just after the pilot applied full right rudder and the right main wheels started its downward swing, the pilot rolled the right wing down approximately 20 degrees and then pulled back sharply on the control column. This caused the right main wheel to swing far enough forward to engage the down lock.

Throughout the whole sequence a crew member was placed at the starboard beam lookout position to inform the pilot of the movement of the right bogey.

Fortunately, Major Field was able to get the gear to lock down by his experimentation and persistence in the yaw manoeuvres. His determination and diligence in doing so saved an Argus aircraft from serious damage and the crew from injury.

Gear Collapse

Technicians were doing engine run-ups when the starboard gear came up. At the time, run-ups were done without the gear pins in place. That changed after this incident.

Photos: Tom Gosling

North Atlantic Rescue

Drama took place on September 27 1970 when Mr. Geigl, a private pilot, filed a VFR flight plan from Sydney, NS to St John's, NL. He got airborne in his Beechcraft *Musketeer* and headed east, outrunning deteriorating weather from the west. Low cloud and fog, which was predicted, block his path approaching Newfoundland so he tried to get below the leather. By this time he had discovered that his navigation was unreliable, requiring some visual reference to fix his position.

At 300 feet altitude over the sea and with only hundreds of yards of visibility, Mr. Geigl found himself flying up small coves and narrowly missing surrounding hills while conducting hasty retreats. Knowing that his situation was hazardous and not likely to improve, he elected to climb in an attempt to get assistance from Air Traffic Control. He contacted Gander Center but they were unable to pick him up on radar. An Air Canada flight tried to assist to no avail. The *Musketeer* was now above cloud at 13,000 feet and in no immediate danger except for a diminishing fuel supply.

A 404 Squadron Argus piloted by Captain Buck Harley and crew were approaching St John's while transiting from Scotland to Greenwood. They had been listening to Gander Centre and were aware of the plight of the *Musketeer*. They offered assistance and Gander Centre immediately cleared the *Argus* to climb above clouds in an attempt to find the lost aircraft.

Captain Harley established VHF communication with a lost aircraft and after some discussion determined it was probably west of St John's. He then directed the pilot, Mr. Geigl, to fly an easterly heading while the Argus carried out a search for him. Captain Gary Thompson soon picked up the *Musketeer* on radar using IFF and then directed the Argus on an intercept course. Twenty minutes later, Captain Ed Swift spotted the light aircraft from the lookout position.

The intercept now complete, a shepherding act followed to St John's, which was 90 miles to the southeast. The tension of the moment was eased and Mr. Daigle was able to complete an instrument approach to St John's with precious little fuel remaining. Captain Harley and crew turned the Argus west again and resumed their transit to Greenwood.

The story might have ended here except for the thankful gestures of the rescued pilot. He had maintained a correspondence with the squadron and offered a monetary reward for his rescue. As this could not be accepted, he made several donations to charitable organizations in Canada and the United States on behalf of 404 squadron.

On December 13, 404 Squadron invited Mr. Geigl of the Merit Tool and Die Company of Hartford, Connecticut to attend the squadrons annual Christmas party and to meet the crew responsible for rescuing him from a very hazardous situation over Newfoundland.

A painting by Jeff Bennet depicts the rescue

Air Shows and Formation Flying

The *Argus* was a very popular aircraft at the many airs shows it participated in throughout North America and overseas. When it first entered into service, the *Argus* was the most advanced ASW aircraft in the world, impressing the many visitors that toured the inside during static displays. Even more impressive was when it did a flying demonstration, especially given its size. This great metal beast would roar in at high speed with lots of noise, do tight combat turns at 500 feet with the two large bomb bays open and perform the "whisper pass" that was probably its most

unique demonstration. The aircraft would approach the show line at high speed and pull the power back on all four engines, passing in front of the crowd with only the wind noise of the aircraft going by to be heard. The *Argus* also participated in fly pasts for special events like change of commands and memorial services. To see these large aircraft in formation was unforgettable.

Eight ship formation of Summerside's 415 Squadron over Greenwood

Photo: Peter Mawle

Formation of Greenwood Argus. This photo was taken by a T-33 chase plane.

Photo: DND

Argus Deployments

Over the years the Argus was deployed to many places around the world and the stories of these deployments could fill a book on their own. From Greenland to Australia, Alaska to Brazil and every country in Western Europe, the Argus made an appearance but perhaps the most visited place was Bermuda. Below is a photo of a major exercise in Bermuda that not only included the Argus but CF100s, CF104s, T33s and S2 Trackers.

Photo: 415 Squadron Collection

415 squadron deployed to Gibraltar in 1970. Note the RAF Hawker Hunters in the bottom left corner of the airfield used to escort both RAF Shackleton MR and CAF Argus

Photo: 415 Squadron Collection

During the many NATO exercises the Argus found itself partnered with many other ASW aircraft such as this German Atlantic

Photo: 415 Squadron Collection

A very unique picture of 415 Squadron's Argus 719 being escorted by two RAF Hawker Hunters during a NATO exercise in the Eastern Atlantic Ocean off the coast of Gibraltar

Photo: 415 Squadron Collection

Argus 742 sits on the apron at CFB Summerside just weeks away from her official retirement. While the CP-140 Aurora, a variant of the P-3 Orion would replace her, the Argus' rough warrior and bomber looking qualities would not be.

Photo: Gary W. Arsenault

The last Argus to leave Greenwood was 736 on July 24, 1981 and to mark the occasion there was a massive parade and a farewell flypast as it winged its way to Summerside.

Photos Above: Greenwood Aviation Museum Collection,

Right and Below: Bert Campbell

The Last Flights

While there are a number of last flight stories, all of which rightly claim a spot in the Canadian aviation history books, official records show that the last "operational" flight of an Argus took place on Monday, November 10, 1980 by a 405 Squadron crew commanded by 405 Squadron Commanding Officer, Lieutenant Colonel Ernie Cable and accompanied by Greenwood Base Commander, Colonel Al McLellan. The last official "non-operational" CP-107 Argus flight occurred on February 10, 1982 when Argus 742, leapt into the sky destined for the Canadian Aviation Museum in Ottawa. The Argus crew was led by Detachment Commander—LCol Jim Lambie, Pilot—Major Wayne Griffith, Co-pilot—Major Mert Rose and Flight Engineers—Chief Warrant Officer Eric Weatherbie and Captain Spike Allen. On the way they did a low-level pass over the Canadair plant in Cartierville, near Montreal, where the Argus was built. Prior to proceeding to Rockliffe, the crew carried out a few practice landings at the Ottawa International airport. On arrival at Rockliffe, 742 carried out a number of low approaches and overshoots while awaiting the arrival of General Hy Carswell.(not because the task of landing on such a short runway was difficult). On landing at Rockcliffe they were met by the recovery crew from CFB Ottawa, Master Warrant Officer W. Anjowaki, Master Corporals George White and J. Rivart and Privates M. Strasbourg and K. Pastetka. Their task was to complete the post light checks and button up the aircraft for the last time.

Argus 742 flies over the Canadair plant in Montreal enroute to Ottawa and the National Aviation Museum

Photo: Wayne Griffith

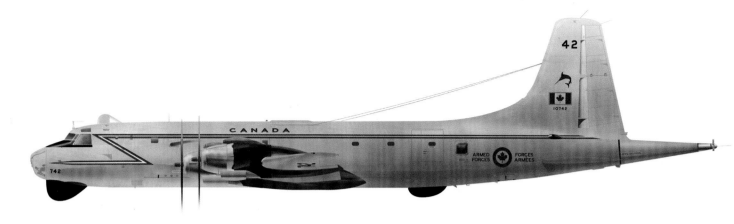

The following Arival message was sent from Ottawa:

SUBJECT: ARRIVAL MESSAGE – END OF AN ERA
AIRCRAFT;   ARGUS 10742
CAPTAIN: MAJ GRIFFITH
ARRIVED: ROCKCLIFFE
DEPARTED: NO FURHTER DEPARTURES. JOHN 17-4* REFERS
STATUS: SERVICEABLE. LAST FLIGHT 4 DECIMAL 6 FLIGHT HOURS
REMARKS: THE ARGUS ERA ENDS. TO ALL AIRCREW, GROUNDCREW AND
             SUPPORT PERSONNEL BOTH MILITARY AND CIVILIAN WHO
             HAVE FLOWN, MAINTAINED, CURSED AND LOVED THIS
             AIRCRAFT OF A THOUSAND EYES, WE ASK YOU TO PAUSE
             SILENTLY FOR A MOMENT AT YOUR NEXT FRIDAY NIGHT
             GATHERING TO RAISE YOUR GLASS IN A FINAL SALUTE AND
             FAREWELL. SHE SERVED US WELL. SHE HAS EARNED THE
             RIGHT TO REST, IN A PLACE OF HONOUR, IN OUR NATION'S
             CAPITAL. AD METAM.
             BT

* NOTE: JOHN 17-4—I HAVE GLORIFIED THEE ON THE EARTH: I HAVE FINISHED THE
WORK WHICH THOU GAVIST ME TO DO.

Where They Are Now

The Mighty Argus is no more, the unmistakable roar of her engines as she took flight are now quiet, her majestic throne in the sky skimming above the waves is just a memory. Once officially retired, those not destined to stand as gate guards or find rest in a museum were cut apart savagely by a scrap company in PEI in 1982 in an act reminiscent of the ill-fated Avro Arrow in 1958. Those that survived now stand alone in various condition around Canada. CFB Greenwood, NS and Comox, BC are guarded by Argus 717 and 712 respectively. Argus 732 sits amid several other aircraft at the CFB Trenton museum. A freshly painted Argus 739 in Summerside sits at the entrance of Slemon Park Airfield (the old CFB Summerside) adorned with a newly emblazoned Sydney Swordfish on her tail, her honour restored by a small group of volunteers known as the "Friends of Summerside Aircraft Preservation Project". Argus 742, which made its last historic flight in 1982 to Rock Cliff airport in Ontario, now sits faded in a new hanger at Canada's National Aviation Museum after almost 30 years of sitting in the wind, snow, rain and sun, hoping that one day she, too, will be restored to her former glory.

As for the other Argus's that could not find refuge from the scrap yard blow torch, each aircraft still lives in the respective memories of the men and women who flew and maintained them. And for us who just couldn't help ourselves from stopping while walking or driving to admire one as she took off and flew overhead, departing for a Search and Rescue mission or returning for landing from another long submarine hunt, she will live on in all her glory.

Argus 742 extends her flaps for the last time as she approaches Rockcliff airport, the location of the National Aviation Museum and her final resting place in Ottawa, Ontario

Photo: Wayne Griffith

The last flight of the mighty Argus is concluded as 742 is welcomed to the Canadian Aviation Museum in Ottawa

Photo: George Mayer

The remaining Argus not destined for gate guard or museum duty await their final end in Summerside, P.E.I

Photo: Gary H. Baker

Gate Guards

Right: A very faded 742, after almost 30 years of sitting outside, finally gets a place in the new National Aviation Museum hangar
Photo: George White

Left: 717 Gate Guard in Greenwood, Nova Scotia
Photo: Greenwood Aviation Museum Collection

Below: 712 Gate Guard in Comox, B.C
Photo: Greenwood Aviation Museum Collection

Right: 739 Gate Guard in Summerside, P.E.I
Photo: Gary W. Arsenault

Below: 723 Gate Guard in Trenton, Ontario
Photo: Greenwood Aviation Museum Collection

And for those of us who just couldn't help ourselves from stopping while walking or driving to admire one as she took off and flew overhead departing for a Search and Rescue mission or returned for landing from another long submarine hunt, she will live on in all her glory.

Probably the most famous picture of the CP-107 Argus 736 being piloted by Captain Gary Baker as she flies over PEI

Photo:DND

Throughout its era, many photos were taken of the CP-107 Argus depicting its undeniable majesty. There are far too many for one single book. This chapter is dedicated to displaying those photos that we felt were a must-see for readers.

This unique photo, taken on 17 Feburary 1959 shows a Golden Hawks Aerobatic Team F-86 Sabre aircraft with the proposed Gold paint job with a T33 and Argus 713 in the background

Photo: DND

Captain Spike Allan, Flight Engineer, greets the welcoming committee in Rockcliffe with Argus 742 after completing her last flight

Photo: George Mayer

Painting: Rob Arsenault

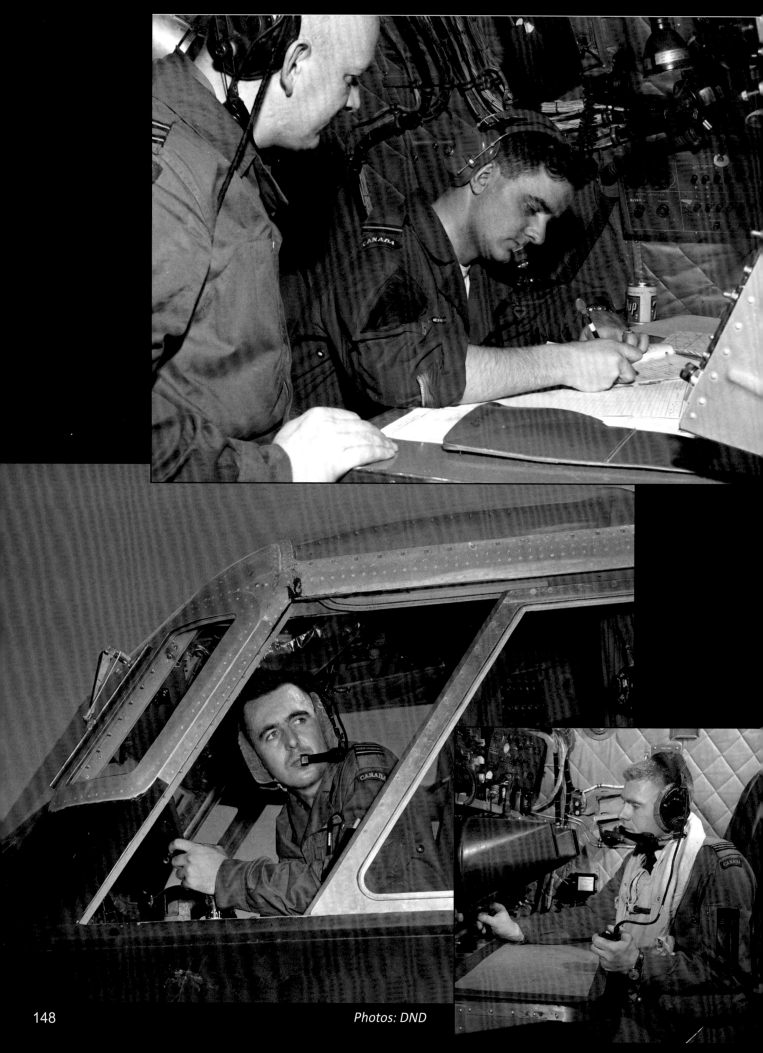

148

Photos: DND

Argus being refueled in Greenwood, Nova Scotia while an H21 Search and Rescue helicopter comes in for a landing

Photo: DND

Photo: George Mayer

Servicing the Argus while on deployment in Bermuda

Photo: 415 Squadron

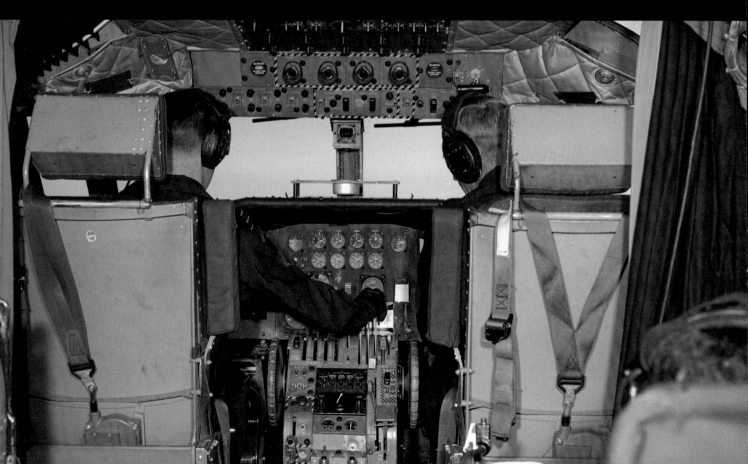

Photos: DND

415 Sqn Argus 739 starts up in RAF Kinloss, Scotland. Captain Gary H Baker was one of a select few Argus pilots who also served as an exchange pilot on the Nimrod MR2 maritime reconnaissance aircraft based at RAF Kinloss

Photo: 415 Squadron

Cpl B.M. Velemirovich is kept busy during a detachment to Bermuda maintaining the correct sonobuoy load in each Argus in 1971.

Photo: 415 Squadron

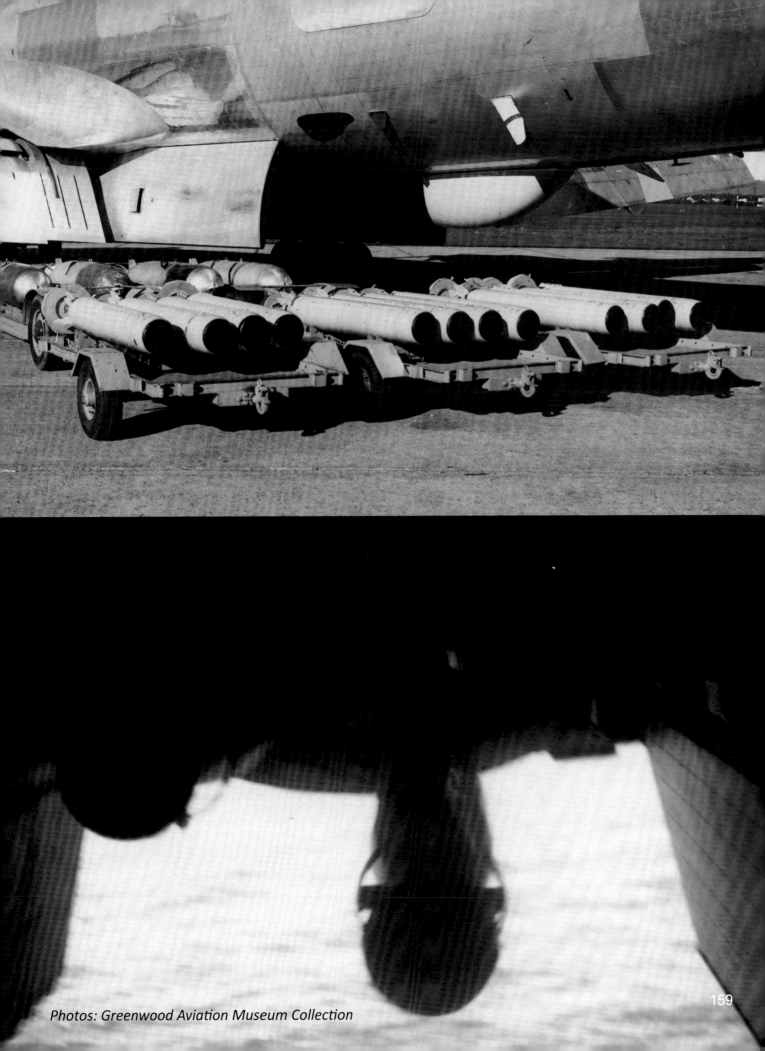

159

161

Photo: 415 Squadron

CF-104 Starfighter and Argus 716 at RCAF Station Uplands, Ontario June 3, 1960

415 Squadron's Argus 736 does her final Greenwood flypast

Photo: Bert Campbell

Three generations of Canadian Maritime Patrol aircraft

Photo: DND

167

Photos: DND

Photo: Pat Boulanger

170

Photo: Gary Arsenault

Photo: Greenwood Aviation Museum Collection

Photo: DND

Photo: Greenwood Avaition Museum Collection

AUSTRALIAN FLIGHT 1973.

VPCC — Capt. PL Murphy

DET. COM. — Maj. DA Little

A Proclamation!
by His Oceanic Majesty King Neptune

WHEREAS it is Our Pleasure to welcome all Adventurous Spirits whose Flights bring them across the Equator

AND WHEREAS We have permitted

106·906·779 Maj. DA Little

to CROSS THE LINE during this Flight whilst serving on

CP 107 Argus 10721

and he, having been duly initiated

WE DO THEREFORE Proclaim him to be a Loyal Subject of Our Domain and he may henceforth be known as a SHELL BACK and this Royal Warrant is issued in substantiation thereof

FURTHER, We require all Lubbers of Air, Sea or Land, all Tritons, Dolphins, Goonies and all others of Our trusty Sea Servant to render him the respect that is his due.

Given at Our Court held on the Equator in Longitude 170° West this 16th day of May, 1973.

Neptunus Rex

180

The prototype Canadair CL-28 Mk 1 (military designation CP-107) Argus aircraft as it appeared at Canadair's Cartierville, Quebec assembly plant. This initial (unofficial) Argus marking scheme featured a non-standard, quad reversing fuselage flash and 405 "Eagle" Squadron's early VN unit code. The APS-20 search Radar was housed in the very large chin fairing. Not all fairings had been installed at this point in time.

In 1971, '724 was adorned with the world famous AETE 'X' clearly depicting a 'Test and Evaluation' (T&E) airframe. This aircraft originally served in Summerside with the Maritime Proving and Evaluation Unit but finished her career at CFB Greenwood.

10728 recently kitted with the APS-94D Side Looking Airborne Radar (SLAR). The 24 foot long antenna was mounted below Starboard rear bomb bay door, which was disabled during the trials. The aircraft was borrowed from 415 Sqn. The unapproved (and shortlived) Roadrunner motif under the Pilot's windshield was applied by a contractor in Arizona.

Profile Drawings: Rob Arsenault

Argus 729 after moving to Greenwood on 08 Aug 1978 in the final MPEU scheme

Another West Coaster, 722 also served previously in both Greenwood and Summerside. The Artist visited the Argus scrap line in 1982 to buy a Nav Seat from 10725 and a Demon prop spinner from the scrapper. While he was there he noticed the men and women from Comox had applied a non-standard marking to 722. Black stripes were added to the Yellow Spinners to make an interesting, and puzzling, Bumble Bee look!

Argus Mk II formerly with MPEU, now with 405 "Eagle" Sqn, CFB Greenwood, NS circa 1978

Profile Drawings: Rob Arsenault

The Argus was Canada's first maritime aircraft to be designed and built in Canada. The aircraft was an unqualified success from the very beginning because of the focused commitment of the people who managed the procurement program as well as those who maintained and flew the aircraft operationally. The excellent relationship between Canadair and the RCAF was the basis of an iterative process of design and comment that resulted in a final product that met all of the RCAF's operational requirements. In view of Canadair's previous experience being limited to manufacturing American aircraft, the company merits special recognition for its entrepreneurial spirit. Canadair embarked on the design and manufacture of the Argus despite its lack of previous design experience in such an extensive program. Canadair successfully managed the risks of incorporating emerging technologies in the Argus, particularly the heretofore-insurmountable technical challenges in the design of the electrical system.

The Argus' finest hour in North American defence and, indeed for world peace, was its key role in defusing the Cuban missile crisis. It was the only allied maritime aircraft that had the range and endurance to patrol the critical sub-air barrier between Newfoundland and the Azores. This contribution is all the more noteworthy when it is considered that Canadian participation lacked political authority and occurred clandestinely under the guise of a national exercise. The Argus' ability to react rapidly and tirelessly in the search for Soviet submarines and ships demonstrated Canada's military resolve to stand shoulder to shoulder with its American ally in times of adversity.

The RCAF retired the Argus in 1981, ending an era in which the uniquely Canadian Argus had proven, both technologically and operationally, to be a maritime world champion.

— *Colonel (Retired) Ernie Cable OMM, CD*

Mighty Argus 10742

By George White

Oh "Mighty Argus", aged and slow
When duty called, over the oceans you would go.

North, South, East or West
There could be no better, you were the best.

From home base to lands far away
You served your country well, day after day.

Through all kinds of weather, bad or good
You did your job, as an ASW aircraft should.

No more "wet power" or commands like that
For your excellent performance, we all tip our hat.

To all your crews, you were just great
Now you have a new home, inside Rockcliffe's gate.

As you sit with poise and grace
A thousand curious eyes, I'm sure that you will grace.

Now serve as a lasting reminder, so majestic and true
Oh "Mighty Argus", known by us all as 742.

Eulogy

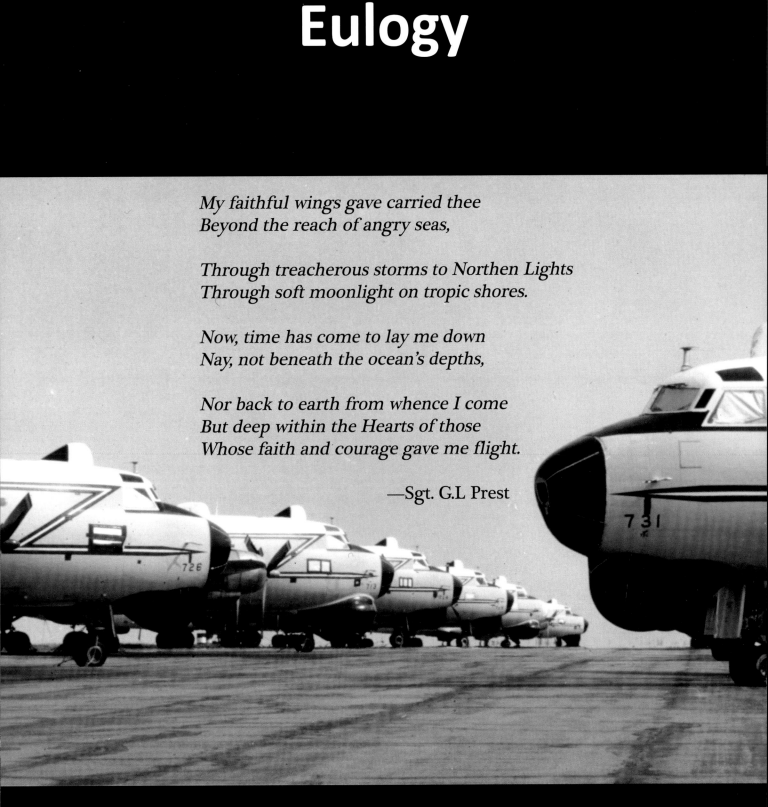

My faithful wings gave carried thee
Beyond the reach of angry seas,

Through treacherous storms to Northen Lights
Through soft moonlight on tropic shores.

Now, time has come to lay me down
Nay, not beneath the ocean's depths,

Nor back to earth from whence I come
But deep within the Hearts of those
Whose faith and courage gave me flight.

—Sgt. G.L Prest

In loving
VP415 C

ry of Captain Gary H. Baker

"Gropers" Aircraft Captain

Illustration: Rob Arsenault

CANADA

736

Acknowledgments

This book would not have come about without the contributions made by many people across Canada. In particular, Colonel (Retired) Ernie Cable who allowed us to use his paper *"Argus - The RCAF's Maritime Champion"* as the frame work for the book, the National Defence Image Library for their time and energy in providing many high quality photographs, The Greenwood Aviation Museum and Rob Arsenault for the outstanding Argus graphics. Over 50 people provided additional photographs, information and stories that were invaluable to the making of this book. They include: Gary Arsenault, Ed Ball, George Baptie, John Belleville, Geoff Bennett, Doug Beaman, Doug Bertram, Pat Boulanger, Denis Boychuk, Ed Bryson, Brian Cameron, Chris Charland, Walt Crocker, Al Currie, Bob Currie, Gerry Dean, Bob Desrochers, Ed Dodd, Norm Donovan, George Doucette, Jim Eakins, Scott Eichel, Andre Elieff, Stefan Elieff, Dave Fletcher, Frank Fletcher, Bob Gaede, Reg Garnett, Moe Gates, Bruce Gormley, Tom Gosling, Lloyd Graham, Wayne Griffith, Ken Hamilton, Tom Hildreth, Bernie Hogan, Peter Holmes, Dwight Houser, Wally Kirkwood, George Kulka, Michel Lafleur, Dave Larken, Debora Lasouski, EJ Lewis, Don Little, Jim Loring, Capt John Low, Barrie MacLeod, Bob MacLeod, Pat Martin, Peter Mawlo, George Mayer, Melaine MacKinnon, Bill McKenzie, Larry Milberry, John Murphy, Darrel Mewman, Ed Olscamp, Col Paul Ormsby, Ian Patrick, Jerry Proctor, Mark Prouix, Paul Roy, Carl Ryan, Pete Sayers, Randy Schroeder, Steve Shea, Paul Skory, Trish Salter, Terry Small, Ian Snow, Richard Sopczak, Derek Squire, Andy Stephaniuk, Richard Stojak, Peter Taggart, Roger Thompson, Mike Vacheresse, Marc-André Valiquette, Leif Wadelius, George White, Dave Wightman, Eric Wood, Ken Wright, Sgt Carrie Joy & Sgt Martine Morin and Craig MacAusland.

Visit the Argus web site at www.cp107argus.com

DND images were reproduced with the permission of the Minister of Public Works and Government Services.

Passing the ASW torch. A CP-107 Argus from 407 Squadron flies in formation with a new CP-107 Aurora in 1980.

Photo: DND